GW00584608

ORIGINAL
TRIUMPH TR

ORIGINAL
TRIUMPH TR

Bill Piggott

Photography by Paul Debois

Edited by Mark Hughes

Published 1991 by Bay View Books Ltd
13a Bridgeland Street
Bideford, Devon EX39 2QE

© Copyright 1991 by Bay View Books Ltd

Designed by Peter Laws

Typeset by Lens Typesetting, Bideford

ISBN 1 870979 24 9
Printed in Hong Kong

CONTENTS

Introduction

Writing this book has proved to be a somewhat larger and more onerous task than I originally envisaged, but no less enjoyable for that. There is a generic similarity running right through the TR line, from the earliest TR2s to the final North American specification TR6s – indeed there are even some parts in common. Because of this similarity, it was felt desirable to cover all these TRs in one book rather than two, even though the total number of cars made handsomely exceeds that of any model previously covered in this series, and the cars were in production for a much longer period – some 23 years.

These facts, coupled with the inevitable limitations of space, have meant that the minutiae of certain specification changes simply cannot be covered in absolute detail, especially for the later models where safety and emission-control equipment began to proliferate. Reproduction factory parts catalogues and manuals are available to elaborate on the more esoteric and arcane details of these cars. Even if totally accurate records existed, which they do not, a book listing every specification change would be both immense and irretrievably dull. What I have tried to do, therefore, is to include all the significant and interesting changes likely to be of most help to those rebuilding their TRs to the highest standards of condition and originality.

As has frequently been stated, there is no such thing as a totally original car – rather that some cars are more original than others. Specifications sometimes changed even on the production line at short notice due to extraneous circumstances or shortages. The question of what is meant by 'originality' in this context is a vexed one, and is the subject of many hours of debate within the more serious car clubs.

Using contacts in the TR Register, we located for photography cars that were, wherever possible, original in that they had not undergone any major restoration work, even if that meant that their condition might not be quite a match for a newly-finished and totally rebuilt concours car. Inevitably, it did not prove possible to assemble a 'full-set' of such cars at the time when they were required for photography, so a few of the cars pictured are in fact rebuilt vehicles – but carefully selected to be as authentic as possible. Any deviations from originality are dealt with in the captions.

I must at this point thank most warmly the photographer, Paul Debois, who, despite inclement weather on several occasions, has managed to produce an excellent gallery of photographs. A few photographs from other sources are individually credited.

I cannot claim that this book is definitive and free of errors. The subject is vast, and the potential for detailed nit-picking is huge. I have tried, with help from the many experts mentioned later, to make it as accurate as possible, but I have to stress that the responsibility for any mistakes is solely mine. What I hope has been achieved is the assembly for the first time in one place of detailed information vital to the TR restorer.

This information, some of it previously unpublished, has been drawn from a variety of sources, but the principal among these is the records held by the British Motor Industry Heritage Trust. I must thank the staff of the Trust generally, and its Archivist, Anders Clausager, in particular, for making me welcome at their premises, allowing me unrestricted use of their records and dealing patiently with my queries. Anders' help with the sections on colours and production figures was of immense value, and has facilitated the compilation of what I hope are the most accurate details yet published on these aspects of TR history.

Writing on such a complex subject teaches one never to be categorical, and subsequent research could well mean that even these sections may not prove to be definitive. But then isn't part of the fascination of the subject the fact that one can never reach the end? It could never have occurred to those who designed and built these cars 30 and 40 years ago that anyone would be interested in the minor details of specification changes all these years later, so matters are frequently not as well recorded as one

would have liked. Nevertheless, the work of the BMIHT has proved invaluable in collecting, conserving and making available such records as have survived.

Although I have been the Principal Registrar of the TR Register for more than a dozen years now, I am neither a professional writer nor a professional car restorer. Consequently, I have drawn on the assistance of a multitude of others in compiling this book, and due thanks must be given.

Following the successful formula established by previous books in this series, a one-day seminar was organised at which eight TR experts viewed, vetted and selected the photographs, discussed the originality points involved and debated TRs generally. These people, who so generously gave up their time, were Roger Ferris, Alec Pringle, Ian Gibson, Peter and Keith Wigglesworth, Neil Hawtin, Ian Cornish and Anders Clausager. In addition, the TR2/3/3A/3B section of the manuscript was read and amended by Ian Gibson, whose knowledge of these cars is unrivalled in my experience. The TR4/4A/5/6 section was read and amended by Roger Ferris (TR4/4A Registrar of the TR Register) and Peter Wigglesworth (long-time TR parts expert from Cox & Buckles Spares, now Moss Motors). Thank you, gentlemen! Neil Hawtin and Roger Ferris also contributed invaluable information on the TR6s and TR4/4As respectively.

As to the cars themselves, thanks are due to the following owners for generously allowing their vehicles to be photographed: Tom Davenport (black long-door TR2), John Hopwood (red short-door TR2), Ken Rawson (TR3), Peter Claxton (red TR3A), Martin King (green TR3A), David Price (red TR4), Derek Pollock (green TR4), Ken Westwood (TR4A), David Bishop (TR4 Dove and TR250), David Tomlin (TR Italia), Andy Mitchell (TR5), Tony James (blue TR6) and Eric Barrett (red TR6). Thanks are also due to those several people who responded to my requests for original cars but whose vehicles we were unable to use, and also to Geoff and Sheila Mansfield of the Northern TR Centre for making the TRs on view in their showroom available for photography at very short notice.

The staff at the ever helpful, friendly and efficient TR Register office, led by Rosy Good, deserve much thanks, as does Ginny Soden (editor of the club magazine), Keith Wigglesworth (club archivist) and Peter Wigglesworth for the loan of irreplaceable

literature. All TR enthusiasts owe a continuing debt to Graham Robson for his invaluable original research; his books are my constant companions. Thanks also to Geoffry Goodall and to Glen Hewett of Protek Engineering, as both made cars available for detailed checking at short notice.

To my editor, Mark Hughes, much thanks are due for his patient and understanding support and advice throughout, and both to him and to Charles Herridge, the publisher, for firstly having the courage and faith to commit this project to my hands, and secondly for not harrassing me over deadlines when the unexpected length of the manuscript caused delays. The book has turned out to be much longer than originally envisaged – yet Charles's gentlemanly letters have always been a delight to read!

If I have left anybody out whom I should have thanked, then I apologise profusely, but final words of thanks are due to my friend and former secretary, Liz Coupe, for so ably reading my terrible writing and typing the manuscript, and to my friend, Karen Nadin, for her help with proof-reading and for her encouragement when I looked like stalling.

By way of explanation, I should say that throughout the book the term 'TR5' should

be read to include the North American specification 'TR250', 'TR6' to include both fuel-injected and carburettor cars and 'TR3A' to include 'TR3B', all unless the contrary is indicated or the context requires otherwise. Concerning the sections on production figures and production changes in relation to the TR2/3/3As, some of the information in this book conflicts with that given in my earlier TR2/3/3A Super Profile, published by Haynes. This is because additional records and information have since become available, and in the case of any conflict the information herein should prevail.

Finally, may I express the hope that if the information in this book leads to more TRs of all sorts being rescued, accurately restored and above all driven, then I feel it will have served its purpose. The TR is, and always was, a driver's car, more so than most of its contemporaries. Properly restored, it is still a safe, rapid and enjoyable means of transport – long may it remain so!

Bill Piggott
Nottingham, April 1991

TRs Past and Present

Tom Davenport's exceedingly original TR2 is a very early long door car, commission number TS477. It still wears its original black paint and has 'Geranium' interior trim, which has faded to a salmon pink. Tom has owned this car almost from new.

The TR series of sports cars grew from the modest origins of the marriage of an essentially pre-war saloon car chassis with a beefy engine destined to power a tractor. To say that this is a simplification is an understatement, yet this is how the prototype was cobbled together at the start of 1952.

At the head of Standard-Triumph in the post-war period was Sir John Black, an industrialist of the traditional, autocratic type. He knew what he wanted, and he wanted it yesterday! Sir John wanted a sports model in his range of cars, and Sir John wouldn't be beaten. William Lyons had produced his Jaguar XK120 and Nuffield was doing well with the MG 'T' types, yet Black's first attempt to enter the lucrative, dollar-earning, sports car market had resulted in the Triumph 1800/2000 Roadster. This car was more in the tradition of the pre-war *boulevardiers* – lots of show and not much go. It was a worthy and interesting vehicle, but not a sports car. It had virtually no competition success and didn't earn many dollars, so Black tried unsuccessfully to purchase the Morgan Car Company.

Morgan, of course, already produced the traditional type of sports car, but eventually no deal could be struck although the company used the Standard Vanguard engine to power its cars. So a second attempt to produce an in-house design was made by Standard-Triumph, this resulting in the 'TRX'

Roadster, colloquially known as the 'Bullet'. Regrettably, this over-complex machine was no more of a sports car than the Roadster, and the project was cancelled after a period of vacillation. As 1952 opened, therefore, Black was no nearer his sports model than he had been in 1946.

A competition-minded amateur, Ken Rawlings, showed the way by designing and building a sports car using largely Standard-Triumph components, including the Vanguard engine. While it has not to my knowledge been proven that the Standard-Triumph management were influenced by, or even aware of, this car, they nevertheless chose this direction in 1952 – a Vanguard engine in a lightweight chassis clothed with a two-seater body. Costs had to be kept low, for large scale production was not envisaged. In-house parts were to be used where possible, and body styling had to be simple – compound curves were avoided – to keep down tooling costs. Harry Webster was the firm's chief designer given overall responsibility for creating the new Triumph Sports, and Walter Belgrove was the chief stylist. Time was very short, as Black wanted the prototype to be on the stand at the 1952 Earls Court Motor Show, held in October.

A chassis based on a modified Standard 'Flying 9' item was used, with a rear axle and front suspension from the Triumph

This is John Hopwood's original low-mileage 1955 TR2. It frequently competes in classic rallies, hence certain items of non-standard equipment, such as reversing light, stickers, boot rack, padding on grab-handle and the black oblongs in front of the hood-stick cover. Note the later 14½in wiper spindle centres. The wiper blades and headlight units are not original.

Mayflower saloon. The Vanguard engine received moderate development, including the fitting of twin SU carburettors. A four-speed version of the Vanguard gearbox was used. A full-width two-seater body with bolt-on external panels was produced, but this had such traditional sports features as cut-away doors and a spare wheel on the sloping tail section.

Only the one Triumph Sports prototype existed when the car was revealed to the public at the 1952 Motor Show, and it had hardly run for time had been that short. Its debut, however, was overshadowed by the sensationally beautiful Healey 100 sports, which had not only run, but had already been enthusiastically road-tested by *Autosport*. The Triumph attracted reasonable interest and quite a few tentative orders, but it was hardly a show-stopper. Following an equally luke-warm reception from the motoring press when they were allowed to try the prototype after the show, Sir John Black asked Ken Richardson, a development engineer and test driver with BRM, to try it.

Richardson knew a bad car when he tried one – and the new Triumph was bad. Somewhat surprisingly, Black accepted Richardson's opinion and asked him to join the company to develop the car into what it should have been. The story of how successfully and quickly this was done has been told many times. Briefly, a much stiffer chassis frame was provided, brakes were uprated and continuous engine development undertaken. Rear bodywork was modified to include an opening boot, and the spare wheel was re-positioned underneath the boot, accessible through a trap-door. Many further minor modifications were made and the result was the TR2, of which three prototypes were built in the first part of 1953. One prototype, it is believed, incorporated some parts from the original car, which had otherwise ceased to exist. The TR was now becoming a serious sports car, giving 100mph performance and rapid acceleration, but with extraordinary fuel economy – yet all this development by Richardson's team took barely five months.

The revised car was first shown to the public at the Geneva Motor Show in March 1953. In May that year, Sir John Black authorised the famous high speed runs at Jabbeke in Belgium, where the TR2 achieved almost 125mph under observed conditions – truly a staggering speed at the time for a 2-litre car in almost standard form. Public interest built up but unfortunately production did not, for the build schedules and component supplies had had to be hastily revised to cope with the unexpected flow of orders now arriving. The first two production cars were built in July 1953, but over the following months pro-duction increased so slowly that only just over 300 cars had been built by the end of the year.

The TR2 was now as fast as its rival Austin-Healey, but more economical and considerably cheaper. Orders flooded in during the first part of 1954 and a waiting list built up. Even so, the majority of cars were going for export, home enthusiasts having to take what they could get as regards colour and specification. Outright victory on the RAC Rally in March 1954 by Johnny Wallwork, coupled with other successes in that most prestigious event, finally convinced any doubters in the competition fraternally that here at last was the 'do everything' sports car at an affordable price. Racing, rallying, touring, going on holiday, going to work – the TR2 could manage them all, and manage them well. By the end of 1954, a TR2 had become the 'kit' to have for serious rally men, and sales never looked back. At last, Sir John Black's dollar-earning dream had materialised, even if ironically by then he himself had left the company.

Development continued, both of the production car and of competition parts. An excellent competition department had been established at the factory under the direction of Ken Richardson, who had stayed on as a full-time member of staff once his original 're-design' brief had been

Ken Rawson's superbly original, two-owner, late TR3. The car, in my view, is finished in a correct shade of British Racing Green – many of the purported Triumph BRG shades are too dark. The hood stick cover does not match the trim, but nevertheless may still be original to the car as a match was not always achieved.

completed. A team of works cars was established, initially for racing *and* rallying, but after 1956 concentrating on rallies with phenomenal success. In 1954 a team of six cars swept the board in their class in the TT, and the car showed well at Le Mans, in the Alpine Rally, and in the Mille Miglia. In 1955 a team of three cars finished strongly at Le Mans, and in 1956 the works rally cars really became the team to beat. However, this is not the place to detail the full competition success of the TR, for this information can be found elsewhere. Suffice to say, in the period 1954–60 the TR was undoubtedly the world's most successful rally car, and probably the most successful 'off the peg' competition car available to the

man in the street at an affordable price. Export success was such that by 1960 over 90 per cent of all production was going overseas, mainly to North America.

In 1954, the original 'long doors' were deleted in favour of shorter doors that would actually allow one to park next to a kerb, and the stylish hardtop was introduced. The following year, 1955, saw the introduction of the slightly-revised TR3, and in 1956 the TR became the world's first series production car to be fitted with disc front brakes as standard. The TR3 continued in production for two years until September 1957, by which time the company's stylists felt that a facelift was in order, especially in view of the huge success

of exports to North America. Across the Atlantic, it was expected that a car, no matter how successful, ought to have an annual, visual update, if only to impress the neighbours.

This policy led to the TR3A, which sported a full-width radiator grille, unkindly referred to at the time as a 'dollar grin'! Various other changes were made, but the substance or the car remained so similar that it is very difficult to tell from the cockpit whether one is driving a 1953 TR2 or a 1960 TR3A. Engineering development, considerably assisted by the works competition programme, continued to the point where the TR was refined into arguably the most reliable, rugged and competi-

This TR3A is Peter Claxton's fully rebuilt car finished in Signal Red. Notice the TR3A type bumper and overriders, together with the new grille and front apron panel.

This very original 1963 TR4 belonging to Derek Pollock is finished in Conifer Green, also known as Triumph Racing Green. It is sporting two period spotlights and correct 60-spoke painted wire wheels. The 'Surrey' hard top, which provides the perfect compromise between full open motoring (with wind buffeting) and saloon car comfort, was always an extremely popular option.

tive sports car available in the late 1950s. Sales climbed each successive year, peaking in 1959/60.

Fortunately, the Triumph management realised that this growth could not go on for ever, and they appreciated the trend towards more civilised sports cars incorporating such luxuries as winding windows and convertible hoods. Design work, started, therefore, on the TR3A's successor, the body styling brief going to Michelotti of Italy. Triumph saw no reason to change radically the mechanical structure of the car, so the plan was for an entirely new body which utilised the TR3A's running gear as far as possible. The only significant mechanical changes were the incorporation

of rack and pinion steering and the increase in engine capacity to 2138cc.

The new car's introduction proved with hindsight to be timely indeed, for a recession hit the motor industry in 1961 and TR sales slumped dramatically for the first time. Meanwhile, Michelotti had designed a very attractive, modern body for what was to become the TR4, incorporating as an optional extra an ingenious hardtop with a removeable central panel. This new bodywork had such classic lines that even today the TR4/4A/5 series has a timeless beauty which, it has to be said, was absent from the more functional, earlier TRs. The new bodywork inevitably meant that the TR4 weighed more than the earlier car, so per-

formance was no better despite the larger engine. However, sales seemed not to suffer from this comparative lack of urge, the new car acquiring a waiting list during its first year of production. Early TR4s went almost exclusively to the USA, cars not being readily available on the home market until the spring of 1962. Contemporary road tests commented favourably on the new steering and the bodywork, and the TR4 can, with hindsight, be considered a success in all respects.

By the early 1960s, competition was featuring less prominently in Triumph's strategy, but nevertheless a team of four works-modified TR4s was formed in 1962 and campaigned successfully for three sea-

David Price's rebuilt TR4 in Signal Red has a contrasting Surrey hard top in black.

Ken Westwood's late TR4A is finished in Royal Blue. This extremely original car has been owned by Ken since new, and has covered just over 100,000 miles.

Andy Mitchell's beautifully-kept TR5 is finished in New White with hardtop and black trim.

sons. By 1964, however, the four-cylinder engine seemed to be reaching the end of its perceived development (but others have worked wonders with it in the 1980s!) and the TR4 was becoming uncompetitive. After 1964, the TR quietly faded from the competition scene, never to return – the new breed of rally-winning cars was drawn from the ranks of modified saloons. However, it must be said that in North America TRs – and TR6s in particular – continued to be raced with success.

By the mid-1960s, comfort and technological advance were becoming very marketable qualities even in traditional sports cars, so Triumph's engineers decided finally to do something about the restricted rear axle movement that had long caused complaints about rear-end grip. As a result, the TR4A arrived with independent rear suspension based on coil springs and trailing-arm type wishbones – a more sophisticated design than that already in use for Triumph's cheaper Spitfire. A new chassis

design was required to accommodate this change, but most mechanical parts were carried over from the TR4. Although the new rear suspension impressed contemporary road testers, and certainly contributed to improved handling and comfort, there were both cost and complication disadvantages. These led to a conventionally-sprung, non-IRS TR4A being produced, to be sold solely in North America alongside the more expensive IRS model.

Once the TR's handling had been modernised, Triumph's engineers were left with the problem of the car's relative lack of performance. The TR4A of 1965 produced performance figures that were really no better than those for the 1953 TR2, and what had once been a sports car in the very front rank for speed and acceleration had become only average, many mid-1960s saloons being capable of outrunning the TR4A. In retrospect, the TR4A can be seen as something of a 'stopgap' model, and it was not quite the sales success that the earlier cars

had been. Clearly, some urgent action was again necessary to revive sales, and this was taken in the form of another 'stopgap' model, the TR5, which arrived in the autumn of 1967.

A six-cylinder 2½-litre engine was developed for the TR5, and when fitted with Lucas fuel injection – the first British true production car to be thus equipped – it promptly produced 150bhp. Triumph considered that the 'old' body still had a little life left – and nothing new had been developed anyway. This engine more than countered previous criticisms of modest performance, the TR5 becoming one of the fastest cars in its price range. For North America, new anti-pollution regulations meant that the fuel-injected car could not be sold, so the TR250 was developed with a carburettor engine and performance barely better than the TR4A's.

Although modified saloons continued to chip away at the traditional sports car market in Europe, open two-seater sales re-

An original Signal Red Triumph TR250 owned by David Bishop. These cars are rarely seen in the UK, as all were exported (mainly to North America) and built with left-hand drive. Whatever the body colour, all cars had a silver reflective painted nose stripe. Front flashers are red, to North American specification.

Tony James' beautiful 1970 Sapphire Blue CP series TR6 is seen in baronial surroundings.

Eric Barrett's marvellous Pimento Red TR6, a CR series car, is totally original and has covered only 25,000 miles from new. It has always been fitted with a hard top and is seen here in a delightful setting showing off the static negative camber of its rear suspension. Notice the black spoiler that was fitted beneath the front bumper on CR series cars.

mained strong in North America. Triumph therefore considered that sufficient potential was left in the TR concept to justify the new bodywork that would undoubtedly become necessary. As is well-known, the German firm of Karmann was instructed to update the TR4/4A/5 body as quickly as possible, and with the minimum of disturbance to the basic structure. Karmann met the near-impossible timescale imposed on them and produced the TR6, which cleverly retained the existing central section (including windscreen and doors) and inner structure, but with new wings, bonnet, boot, front and rear panels and external trim. The resulting car was handsome and modern-looking, and it was ready for production in late 1968, succeeding the TR5/250 after that model had had a life of only 15 months. With its excellent performance and updated looks, the fuel injected TR6 sold strongly in Europe. The slower North American version with carburettors sold even better, despite progressively having its performance eroded by additional anti-pollution equipment.

The TR6 stayed in production longer than any other TR model, but by the latter stages it was inevitably becoming an anachronism and sales eventually slowed. The company saw no reason to commit further funds in a vain attempt to keep alive a concept whose time had apparently passed, and hence the TR family rather faded away. The last fuel-injected TR6s were made in February 1975, while the North American cars staggered on in strangulated form until July 1976.

Looking back from the 1990s, maybe the subsequent reputation of the TRs would have been better served had production ceased in the early 1970s, before emasculation and de-tuning took place. But who can blame the company for trying to extract the final financial knockings from what had been for more than 20 years one of the world's most successful series of sports cars?

Turning to view the TR scene nowadays, one cannot say that it looks other than healthy. Values have risen substantially over the past few years; in many ways this is a mixed blessing, but it has had the beneficial effect of making restoration more cost-effective, which in turn has led to a considerable proliferation of specialist firms dealing with TR parts and restoration. The parts supply situation, particularly for the 'sidescreen' models, is extremely good. Indeed, it is little exaggeration to say that it would now be possible to create in all substantial respects a new TR3A from scratch!

How different this is from 1970, when early TRs were just scruffy old sports cars being run into the ground by impecunious students and the like, parts usually being provided by the cannibalisation of other similar cars. In that year, the TR Register was formed to act as a support group for TR enthusiasts, and to help track down sources of spares. The success of this organisation, now one of the world's largest one-make car clubs, is one of the principal factors behind the present TR renaissance.

The TR racing scene, too, is extremely healthy, the TR Register's season of 'TR only' races attracting full grids year after year and ensuring that these cars are still used for one of their original purposes – providing competitive motoring at moderate cost. Even the six-cylinder cars, rarely used for competition in the UK when they were current, have been developed into race-winning machines.

In conclusion, it is today possible to restore any TR to a very high standard of originality and condition. But be warned that this can never be an inexpensive exercise; even at today's values, the costs of such restoration will frequently exceed the value of the completed car.

Triumph TR2/3/3A

CHASSIS

As is well known, the original chassis frame under the prototype TR proved inadequate, its rigidity leaving much to be desired. Thus the chassis was considerably strengthened during the winter of 1952-3, while the many faults of the TR prototype were being 'redesigned' out or eliminated by testing and trial and error.

The chassis that eventually reached production consisted of two full-length side members in 15swg steel of roughly 3in × 3½in section, the narrower section being at the top and bottom. These two members are connected at the extreme front by a small diameter cross tube, and then approximately 9in further back by a major cross-member of roughly the same section as the side members. Front suspension towers grow upwards at this point, and at the top are connected by a further tubular cross-member, which can be unbolted to facilitate engine replacement. Front suspension inner wishbone mounting points are situated either side of the suspension towers, and pointing backwards from the top of these towers are strengthening arms, one on each side, which carry body front mounting points.

The main side members, which are parallel at the front, turned outwards just aft of the suspension towers to enable the chassis frame to reach its maximum width about one-third of the way back, roughly in line with the top of the front bulkhead. Just past the point of maximum width, tubular body mounting members are attached, passing through the main chassis members to join with the cruciform bracing that forms the central portion of the frame. There are two sets of such members, the rear ones not quite as wide overall as the front ones. The inner sills of the bodywork are bolted onto flat plates welded to the top of the ends of each of these tubes. Between the two sets of tubular body mounting outriggers, jack mounting sockets are found on the insides of the frame side members.

The frame narrows towards the rear axle area. Just before the axle line is reached, upright flanged plates are welded, one to each side member, to carry the lever-arm rear shock absorbers. These plates had to be strengthened twice early on in the production run, stiffening ribs being incorporated to prevent fracture. The main modification was incorporated at TS 4310; at the same time infill plates were added ahead of the chassis cruciform. The forward ends of the

rear springs are carried on pins which pass through the side members, the idea being that such pins could be extracted in an inwards direction to allow for rear spring removal without having to disturb the bodywork. Unfortunately, years of rust frequently thwart the designers' aims, as too many owners have found to their cost.

The rear axle passes over the side members, a design which restricted wheel movement and contributed to the less than perfect rear end roadholding. Just behind the rear shock absorber mountings, the frame ceases to narrow and becomes parallel for approximately its final 3ft of length. Almost at the same point, the side members turn up when seen in side view, and continue on a 'rising gradient' to the rear of the car. There are usually small drain holes in the base of the side members at this point. Two tubular cross-members of differing strength connect the rear of the frame. The forward one is of narrower section and carries the rear spring shackles at its outer ends, having passed through the centre of the side members. The aft one is roughly 1½in in diameter; where it attaches to the side members at the rear, gusset plates are welded to provide strength and body mounting points.

As described earlier, the chassis has a central cruciform formed of channel section with a central 'box' connecting the two sides of the cruciform. The exhaust system passes through this central box member, and just forward of the box is found a bolted-in gearbox cross-member.

During TR2 production, a further bolted-in 'quasi' cross-member was introduced (at TS 3512) in the form of a radiator protection cross-piece. This became necessary as the bottom of the radiator proved vulnerable to puncture by stones. The front bumper irons are bolted to the forward end of the chassis frame, by two bolts each side; the forward pair of bolts is used also to attach this radiator protection piece. The rear overriders are bolted to the rear body mounting brackets, the upper bolts being angled down through the rear of the bodywork.

The main body is mounted on the chassis at 12 points, six on each side. Three of these are forward of the front bulkhead. There is only a single mounting point at the rear on each side and a central one at the rear of the cruciform bracing. However, the inner sills are also bolted to the tubular outriggers with four bolts on each side, two for each outrigger, and struts connect the trailing

edge of each rear wing with the chassis. The main body mounts have pads of insulating material between body and chassis; this material is also used along the top of the central cruciform in a further attempt to insulate the bodywork from the chassis.

Chassis frames were initially manufactured by Standard-Triumph, but early in production their manufacture was contracted out to Sankey. Frames, it seems, were invariably finished in black, irrespective of the car's body colour.

Other than those already mentioned, changes during production were minimal, being confined mainly to brake and fuel pipe pick-up points and clips, and extra brackets which were added to support the 'split' two-piece steering column introduced during the TR3A's production run.

FRONT SUSPENSION

As was quite common for sports models where relatively low levels of production were envisaged, many mechanical components were borrowed from saloon cars already in volume production within the company's range. The Triumph Mayflower donated the principal components of its front suspension system to the TR, which, of course, eventually considerably outsold its saloon benefactor. For improved strength, however, the pressed-steel Mayflower lower wishbones were replaced on the TR with forged components.

The system is independent, based on coil springs and upper and lower wishbones. The coil springs are held within the suspension towers of the chassis, and telescopic shock absorbers are housed inside the springs. These are removed from the bottom, where they are able to pass through the spring-pan bolted to the lower wishbone arms. The dampers are fixed at their tops to the suspension towers and act on the lower wishbone arms. At the outer end of each top wishbone is a swivelling ball-joint, bolted to a vertical link which connects the top and bottom wishbones and carries the stub-axle. The bottom of the vertical link is threaded, and this threaded portion mates with a bronze trunnion in which it is free to turn within limits, allowing for steering action. The trunnion has pins extending from either side which pass through eyes in the lower wishbones, allowing the rise and fall of the suspension. These trunnions wear rapidly (especially if not greased properly) and are the Achilles

Seen here is the correct steering wheel, horn-push and indicator switch for a TR2. The Lucas plug socket (usually used to accept an inspection lamp) under the speedometer is not original, but is of the period. The instruments and switchgear are correct, but the 'barrel' overdrive flick-switch on the extreme right is not original to an early TR2, which should have a push-pull switch. This type of 'barrel' switch was used on later TR2s and subsequent cars. The rear-view mirror and screen stay are correct, and the chromed bolts used to hold the optional aeroscreens can be seen.

Heel of the suspension. No anti-roll bar was ever fitted as standard, although proprietary types were available and the factory listed one as an optional extra from the start of TR3A production.

King pin inclination is 7 degrees, castor angle is nil, and front wheel camber (static laden) is 2 degrees. Front hubs initially had grease nipples for the wheel bearings, but these were deleted from TS 5348 because enthusiastic over-greasing could cause brake linings to become contaminated; the hubs were strengthened at the same time. Few other changes to the front suspension were found necessary, although the rubber lower inner wishbone bushes were changed to a steel and nylon type at TS 9122, shortly after the TR3 was introduced. These later bushes can be used on the earlier cars, and last much longer.

The introduction of disc brakes also caused very little modification to the front suspension design. The same trunnions and vertical links were used, although the stub axles and hubs themselves differed. Therefore, the conversion of a drum-braked car to discs has presented few difficulties and many such conversions have been performed over the past 30 years or so.

The front springs were not modified. These are of 1/2in diameter wire with 6-3/4 coils each of 3-1/2in diameter. The free length is 9-3/4in with a fitted length of 6-3/4in and a rate of 310lb/in. Factory competition front springs, incidentally, have a rate of 380lb/in and a free length of 9.19in.

The suspension was painted black when new, but shock absorbers were usually left in the manufacturer's colour. Silver, black and red have been seen, so it is impossible to be categorical as to what is correct.

REAR SUSPENSION

The rear suspension design could hardly be simpler. The rear axle passes over the chassis frame and is suspended on a pair of semi-elliptic springs of conventional design. No other locating medium is employed, the axle relying entirely on the stiffness of these springs to keep it in place.

The underslung chassis restricted wheel movement in a vertical direction, and metal check-strap loops were bolted over the axle to restrict upward movement. A rubber bump stop with both an upper and lower face was wired around the axle to engage with the check straps and chassis top face.

The springs have six leaves, and were listed as having a nominal laden camber of 7/8in negative. Their static deflection was given as 4.04in. At their forward ends they are anchored on the removeable pins mounted through the chassis frame side members, and at the rear on shackles which allow for movement under deflection of the spring. Competition specification springs were available, but the standard springs continued unmodified, at least on the driver's side of the car. The factory parts book indicates that from TS 26904, early on

in the TR3A's run, a different spring with a new part number started to be fitted to the passenger side. It may be that a softer spring was introduced on this side in an attempt to compensate for the driver's weight when the car was being driven solo, but this is speculation.

Conventional Armstrong lever-arm shock absorbers were bolted to the brackets on the frame and connected to the spring bottom plates by drop-links. The specification of the shock absorbers appears not to have changed during production, although TR3Bs from TSF 265 used TR4 specification items. The change to the stronger, Girling-braked, rear axle at TS 13046 did not necessitate a change of spring, but new hubs were used. Modified U-bolts and bottom plates were required because the axle casing itself was larger in diameter.

Rear suspension was finished in black.

STEERING

The adjustable cam and lever type steering was made by Alford & Alder, and the ratio was 12 to 1. Steering lock stops were set to allow a turning circle of roughly 32ft, with 2-1/4 turns lock to lock. TR2/3/3A steering is heavy, especially at low speeds and on cars fitted with modern radial-ply tyres. To provide the necessary leverage, there is a large diameter 17in steering wheel manufactured by Bluemels. Front wheel track is 3ft 9in and alignment was specified as

The interior of Martin King's ex-works TR3A rally car, VRW 221, showing an original wood-rim steering-wheel, which demonstrates how the correct type horn-push was incorporated. Also visible are period rally accessories, such as the 'Halda' speed-pilot unit, map light and additional instruments. The seat-piping appears to be somewhat more curved than is usual (Bill Piggott photo).

between parallel and ⅛in toe-in.

The steering box is adjustable by means of a screw and lock nut adjustment on the rocker shaft, and of course tracking is adjustable by turning the internally threaded outer tie-rods. The steering box and column were originally in one piece, but this was later changed. The steering box bolts to a bracket near the front of the chassis frame, and a similar but opposite-handed bracket on the passenger's side supports the steering idler. A central tie-rod supported on 'silentbloc' bushes at each end connects the steering and idler arms, and the outer tie-rods pivot on ball joints from the central tie-rod.

The steering column is very long, and passing through it is a stator tube enclosing the wiring to the control head on the steering wheel, operating the horns and self-cancelling indicators. The horn push is in the centre of the wheel, surrounded by a thin chromed rim; the indicator control is positioned above the wheel hub and normally points straight upwards, deflecting roughly 20 degrees either side for left or right turns.

The steering wheel, which has moulded finger grips on the reverse, is black, as is the control head hub, although some examples in very dark brown have been seen, possibly because the original Bakelite plastic has faded. The standard steering wheel has three wire spokes, each spoke comprising four wires. The spokes are arranged in a 'T' shape: in the straight-ahead position, the

bottom of the 'T' should point directly downwards.

An adjustable steering column was available as an optional extra to give about 3½in more outwards adjustment. Adjustment is effected by a knurled locking ring below the steering wheel hub; to allow for movement, the stator tube is slotted and the splines at the top of the column are considerably lengthened. A quite different steering wheel was provided when adjustable steering was specified. Although still of 17in diameter, its spokes were disposed like a Mercedes-Benz three-pointed star motif. Although each spoke was still formed by four wires, these were positioned in two pairs with a central gap.

Well into the production run, probably in late 1958 but, surprisingly, at a point which cannot be at present identified from the records, the standard one-piece column and steering box was changed for a two-piece split type, presumably to facilitate steering box removal without having to remove the front apron panel.

The steering column and box should be painted black, although the steering idler usually came as an unpainted casting. Left-hand drive cars were always in the majority, the export proportion growing throughout production so that by 1960 only about 5 per cent of cars were being manufactured with right-hand drive.

BRAKES

The prototype TR had been fitted with 9in × 1¾in width Lockheed drum brakes on all wheels, but by the time production began the front brakes had been increased to 10in × 2¼in width (giving a lining area of 148sq in) to cope with the car's greater speed potential.

The brakes are, of course, activated hydraulically. The front brakes on Lockheed braked TRs have two leading shoes, each shoe with an activating cylinder, whereas at the rear one sliding cylinder operates both shoes in each brake. A twin-bore master cylinder is fitted, one bore operating the clutch, the other the brakes. This master cylinder unit is bolted to a pedal box bracket fixed to the front bulkhead. Pendant pedals operate the master cylinder pistons directly. No servo mechanism was specified; although some owners have fitted them, it seems that a servo was never offered by the factory as an option. The fluid reservoir is combined with the master cylinder block, with an internal divider to ensure that the brakes remain unaffected if the clutch fluid leaks away. There are only three flexible hoses in the system: one to each front brake, and a single one from a bracket near a rear shock absorber mounting to the rear axle, from which point solid brake pipes lead to each rear wheel. Mintex linings were used, first of type DM7, then type DM8, and finally the harder type M20.

In competition or hard road use, even the production TR2's uprated system with 10in front brakes proved inadequate, so from TS 5443 the rear brakes were also increased in size to match the 10in × 2¼in dimensions at the front. This certainly improved braking, but it led to rear wheel locking problems which plagued the TR for many years. In addition, when cold, the drum brake system had a disconcerting propensity to 'grab' that was not eliminated until disc brakes arrived.

Brake fade also remained a problem, but this was countered in September 1956 (at TS 13046) when the TR3 became the world's first car in true series production to adopt disc front brakes as standard. This necessitated a complete redesign of the braking system, and the rear axle was also changed. The new brakes were by Girling, with 11in front discs balanced at the rear by those 10in × 2¼in drums. The old twin-bore master cylinder was discarded, the clutch and brakes being given independent master cylinders. In addition, the fluid reservoir was separate, although it still served both brake and clutch systems with an internal divider. Although pedals were now cranked to allow for the greater distance between bore centres, pedal box assemblies remained the same. Detailed changes were made to the brake pipework and bracketry, the flexible hoses, of course, now being of Girling manufacture. The effective area rubbed by the front discs was 248sq in, compared with 87sq in for the rear 10in drums.

Although the adoption of disc brakes cured fade, wheel locking and overbraking at the rear continued. Triumph tried differing sizes of rear wheel cylinders in an effort to overcome this, and details will be found in the 'Production Changes' section. Eventually, however, the solution was found to lie in a return to 9in × 1¾in rear brakes, and these were introduced in 1959 at TS 56377. Being by Girling, these new rear brakes are not interchangeable with the earlier 9in Lockheed items. Concurrent with this change, the latest type of Girling front disc caliper was adopted. This was the 'B' type which split into halves to facilitate service work and manufacture, whereas the earlier type had been a one-piece unit.

The mechanical handbrake operates on both rear wheels and is very efficient if kept in good order. It is fully capable of locking the rear wheels at 30mph, even with 9in rear brakes! This efficiency was partly due to the tremendous mechanical advantage avail-

able from the length of the handbrake lever, which was fitted with a racing-style push button fly-off action guaranteed to confuse youthful MoT testers nowadays!

The handbrake grip is usually in black rigid plastic, but white was also used and I have even heard tell of some in red. Late TR3As used a flexible plastic grip and an unthreaded lever. The lever and its release button are chromed.

Irrespective of which side the steering is fitted, the lever is always fitted to the left-hand side of the gearbox tunnel (when viewing the car from the front). Drivers of right-hand drive TRs will be familiar with the constant rubbing of the left leg against the handbrake! Where the lever passes through the floor it is shrouded by a black rubber boot, and the quadrant-style ratchet mechanism is positioned directly below this point. A single sheathed cable connected to the lever pulls on a compensating bell-crank assembly mounted on a bracket on the rear axle, and from here open cables run to the back of each rear brake drum. Mechanical expanders attached to the rear wheel cylinders cause the shoes to expand and apply the brakes.

Most of the handbrake assembly remained the same after the adoption of Girling brakes, but the brake levers and expanders in the rear brakes were changed to suit the new design of wheel cylinder. Adjustment on Lockheed brakes is by snail-cam adjusters, but the Girling type are adjusted by an inward/outward screw protruding through the backplate, and operating wedges and tappets bearing on the shoes. Disc brakes, of course, are self-adjusting.

When steel wheels were fitted, brake drums were painted black at the factory. However, on cars originally fitted with wire wheels, drums could have either black, aluminium or silver paint. Alfin drums were listed as an optional extra in 9in or 10in form; although TR types usually have 'lateral' cooling fins, some were made for early TRs with circumferential fins. Incidentally, there appears to be a measure of brake drum interchangeability between the Lockheed and Girling systems, for I have found that a 10in Alfin drum taken from the Lockheed front brakes of a TR2 fits perfectly on the 10in Girling rear brakes of a TR3A, and that the original Lockheed 9in rear drum was resurrected for the post-TS 56377 Girling 9in rear brakes!

REAR AXLE

Two distinct types of axle, both derived from saloon cars in the Standard-Triumph range, were fitted to sidescreen TRs.

On cars up to TS 13045, the axle is based on the Mayflower unit, although with a narrower track to suit the TR's reduced width. From TS 13046 onwards, the axle is the much stronger Vanguard Phase 3 type, again adapted to suit the TR. Both axles use the same crownwheel, pinion and differential gears, but the axle tubes, hubs and half-shafts are much more robust on the later type; in addition, taper roller bearings replaced the previous ball bearings.

It has proved almost impossible to break the later axles, and over the years competition-minded TR owners have put through them twice as much power and torque as the designer intended, without ill effects. The same cannot be said of the Mayflower type axle, which was prone not only to half-shaft breakage, even with standard power outputs, but also had weak hubs and poor oil seals which frequently allowed the rear brakes to become soaked in oil. Modified hub oil seals were introduced at TS 5114 and stronger hub nuts at axle number TS 8039. At TS 5556, hub boss diameter increased from 1½in to 1⅝in, seals again being modified to suit. However, the problem was really solved only by the introduction of the later axle.

Both axles are of the hypoid-bevel, semi-floating type, with a detachable rear cover for access to the differential and crown wheel and pinion set. Provision is made for shim adjustment for the differential bearings and end-wise location of the crown wheel. Oil capacity is 1½ pints. The standard ratio is at 3.7 to 1, which conveniently gives almost exactly 20mph per 1000 revs in direct top gear. This is obtained by a 37-tooth crown wheel mating with a 10-tooth pinion. Contrary to the position with many designs, the same 3.7 to 1 ratio was specified even when overdrive was fitted, the torquey engine being more than capable of pulling the resulting 3.03 to 1 gearing – overdrive is thus very much in the nature of a fifth gear.

From the introduction of the TR3, it became possible to specify a 4.1 to 1 ratio in conjunction with an original-fit overdrive unit, but cars so fitted are fairly rare. Some competition-minded owners did on occasions use even lower axle ratios, but the 4.1 ratio was the only alternative offered by the works; even with this fitted a standard

This early TR2 is one of the few which did not have Triumph 'world' medallions on the nave plates. Disc wheels on TR2/3s should always be body colour. Note how the original black paint has almost polished through on the door, which is, of course, the 'long' variety with no outer sill below.

road-going TR feels a touch under-geared, although in-gear acceleration is slightly improved.

Lockheed axles can have two types of hub units. When wire wheels were specified, a modified hub incorporating the wheel-carrying splines was fitted. From the introduction of the Girling axle, separate bolt-on hub extensions were fitted to carry wire wheels, and one type of hub covered both wire and disc wheels. These bolt-on hub extensions can easily be used to convert a Lockheed axle car to wire wheels, the only necessary modification being to shorten the wheel-holding studs.

As with other chassis components, axle casings and hubs should be painted black. Axles are stamped with a 'TS' number in their own series, roughly equating to the car commission number, the number usually being stamped into the top edge of the casing on the opposite side to the breather.

WHEELS & TYRES

Although steel disc wheels were always the standard equipment, knock-on wire wheels were available at extra cost almost from the start of TR2 production. Throughout the sidescreen TRs' production run, only a low percentage (10-15%) of cars were so fitted as built. Owing to fashion and the ease of

The original chromed nave plate fitted to disc wheels, showing the Triumph 'Globe of the World' medallion. These items were used, in very similar form, on disc-wheeled TRs from 1954 to 1967.

retro-fit conversion, however, a much greater percentage of surviving cars is now found with wire wheels.

The disc wheel has 12 brake cooling holes, positioned radially in three groups of four, and was initially of 4J rim width. As soon as people started to race their TR2s, wheel centres gave trouble and fractures occurred, the wheel pulling off its centre with dire consequences in some cases. As a result, stronger wheels of 4½J section were introduced at TS 1869 in May 1954, and up-rated wheel nuts soon followed at TS 1927. These items were made available retrospectively to owners of existing cars, and consequently very few of these early 4J wheels survive – although I purchased TS 494 in 1976 and was amazed to discover that it was still on its original 'thin' wheels! The new, stronger disc wheel must have proved very satisfactory, as no specification change then

This TR3A has 60-spoke painted wire wheels, which were available as an option during the later stages of TR3A production, although 48-spoke wheels were the standard wear. The TR3A's external door handles can be seen; the special 'performance' exhaust silencer and tailpipe are non-original.

appears to have occurred right through to the end of four-cylinder TR production in 1967.

The disc wheel is embellished with a chromed nave plate, in the centre of which is usually found the Triumph 'Globe of the World' medallion, but some of the earliest TRs (including Tom Davenport's very early black car in the photographs) appear to have had these emblems omitted. These nave plates were probably old Mayflower stock being used up! The part number of the medallion changes at TS 13046, at which point the earlier vitreous-enamelled 'globes' were superseded by the painted type, with a slightly altered design. The nave plate pushes onto three studs on the wheel, and to facilitate removal a 'hockey stick' shaped tool was included in the basic tool kit.

There were two types of jack, the second type – and possibly the first as well – being made by B.T.C. Ltd. The first type, used up to TS 5468, had no separate ratchet handle and had a ball-jointed foot. There-after, a ratchet handle was used and the ball-jointed foot was deleted. The jack was of an unusual type in that it engaged in a bracket on the inner side of each main chassis frame member, with access to this bracket via holes in the floor, one each side just forward of the base of the seats; these holes were normally blanked by large rubber grommets, although the earliest cars had steel blanking plates. It was possible to jack the car up, in theory at least, without leaving the seats! The design of these jacks was not wholly satisfactory and not many survive, most owners preferring a more stable conventional screw jack placed under the chassis frame.

The wheelbrace was a $7/8$in AF socket welded to the end of a shaft just over a foot long, with a handle that folded out at right angles to provide sufficient leverage to move the nuts. This item and the nave plate extractor were omitted, of course, from wire-wheeled cars, when a hammer for the knock-off nuts was supplied instead. The hammer was originally hide-faced but a copper-faced item was substituted later – either type could be correct.

Disc wheels on TR2s and TR3s were painted the same colour as the bodywork, but from the TR3A the wheels were finished in a colour described by the factory alternatively as 'silver lacquer' or 'aluminium wheel paint'. It is not certain whether these were two names for the same thing or if the two colours differed. The reference number of CD31568 has been found for the aluminium wheel paint.

Debate has continued for years over whether sidescreen TRs were ever supplied ex-factory with chromed wire wheels. Certainly the later parts books refer to the availability of both 'dull chrome' and 'bright chrome' wires as replacement parts, in addition to the two painted finishes referred to as 'aluminium' and 'lacquer'. It seems that while *chromed* wire wheels were not specifically listed as an option, they could, for an extra payment, nevertheless be obtained as original equipment. There is little doubt that some cars, especially for the USA, were fitted with them from the factory.

The standard wire wheel, manufactured by Dunlop, has 48 spokes (16 long outer ones and 32 shorter inner ones). Although 60-spoke wire wheels were not listed as being available, it is clear from photographs that the works rally cars were frequently using them, so one can presume that these would have been available to a private owner with money to spend. The knock-off nuts were chromed and had no name on them, merely the words 'left' and 'right' as appropriate with an arrow indicating direction of tightening.

If an owner wishes, 60-spoke wire wheels can be retro-fitted onto earlier TRs without clearance problems, and post TS 13046 Rudge type wire wheel hub extensions can be fitted onto a disc wheel car by using the correct $11/16$in AF nuts, the only modification necessary being to shorten the existing wheel studs. Even this has been avoided by some owners, by having 9mm spacers interposed between the splined hub extension and the brake drum, thus allowing an instant conversion back to disc wheels if required.

This TR2 engine view shows the early internal bonnet release mechanism, together with the pre-TS1201 'double' thermostat housing. The air cleaners are correct, but should have a transfer on them regarding maintenance. The battery stays should have wing, rather than plain, nuts. The 1954 windscreen washer bottle suits the period, but was never a standard fitment. The servo unit is non-standard, and is fitted on this particular car to operate the clutch. The flasher unit was moved early on to this position, as it got too hot when mounted lower on the bulkhead. Also, the wiper motor is correctly mounted on this side on this particular car, though it was on the other side on most 'sidescreen' cars.

As initially supplied, sidescreen TRs usually came with Dunlop crossply tyres. The standard size was 5.50 × 15, fitted with inner tubes. However, Dunlop's Road Speed tyres in the same size were offered as an optional extra virtually from the start of production, and many cars were delivered with these covers which are more suitable for the car's speed capability. By 1956, the first radial ply tyres were becoming readily available, and 155 × 15 Michelin X radials were being listed as an option alongside Dunlop Road Speed crossplies. The basic crossply 5.50 × 15, however, still remained the standard fitment even on the early TR3A, although as production progressed the proportion of cars delivered on Road Speeds or radials increased. White-wall tyres were supplied as an option principally on cars sent to the USA, although they could be specified also in other markets.

The nearest crossply equivalent tyre readily available today is a 5-90 × 15, and owners in search of originality would need to make do with these. In any event, the 5.50 × 15 size was superseded by the 5-90 × 15 in 1958 when sizes were rationalised. Crossplies make the steering lighter and fill the wheel arches more appropriately, but they cannot otherwise be recommended for sidescreen TRs, unless the owner wishes to recreate the tail-end happiness for which the

model was once renowned!

These cars handle much better on modern radials, although it is becoming extremely difficult to obtain even these in the original 155 × 15 size. The most widely used size today on sidescreen TRs is 165 × 15, and these further improve roadholding. However, they do have a drawback, because the spare wheel compartment was designed for the earlier sizes. While a disc wheel fitted with a 165 × 15 tyre might *just* go in, a wire wheel with such a tyre will usually refuse, except on a post-TS 60001 TR3A, which had a modified spare wheel well to cope with larger tyres. To overcome this difficulty, one can either keep a 155 radial, if obtainable, as a spare (but this may be of doubtful legality) or keep the spare wheel with its 165 tyre deflated (when it *will* go in) and carry a foot pump!

ENGINE

Much has been made over the years of the TR having a 'tractor' engine: although this engine was used in various forms for many years in the Ferguson tractors manufactured by Standard-Triumph, this was not its intended use when conceived.

Following the end of the war in 1945, the company, under Sir John Black, realised

that a new engine of approximately 2-litres would be needed to power the all-new saloon car then being developed, and Ted Grinham, the Technical Director, was briefed to oversee its design and development. This saloon car became the Standard Vanguard, and arguably its best feature was this rugged new engine. The lengthy story of how a strong but not obviously sporting motor was painstakingly developed into the unit in the TRs has been well told elsewhere, so I will confine myself to descriptive details.

The TR engine is of wet-liner construction: the pistons run not directly in the block, but in individual cylindrical liners which are removeable. The liners are surrounded as far as practicable by a water-jacket that is sealed at the top by the head gasket and at the bottom by 'figure of eight' gaskets. The advantages of such construction are better cooling, the ease with which worn liners can be replaced (simply by being pressed in), and the simplicity with which engine capacity can be changed (just by fitting a set of pistons and liners of different bore sizes). The liners are of nickel-chrome iron, and the flat-topped pistons, made of aluminium alloy, are fitted with two compression rings and one oil scraper ring.

The standard capacity is 1991cc, with

The air cleaners are correct on this TR3, but would have had transfers indicating maintenance procedure. The wiper motor has changed sides compared with the TR2, which is correct. Non-original items in this view are the plastic screen-wash bottle, red paint on the dynamo pulley and heater tap, the black covering on the fuel lines to the carburettors, the packing around the battery, the car alarm on the bulkhead and the 'pegboard' on the inner wings. Note the body number plate, stamped from brass, visible above the left-hand battery terminal.

83mm bore liners and a 92mm piston stroke, a compression ratio of 8.5 to 1 being used. For export markets, a compression plate could be employed to reduce the ratio to 7.5 to 1. Following their use in works rally cars, 86mm liners and pistons later became available to give 2138cc.

The block is made of cast iron with a sheet steel sump fitted underneath (although a cast aluminium sump was optionally available). The crankshaft is carried by three main bearings, which, like the big end bearings, feature precision-machined, steel-backed, white metal bearing shells. The crankshaft itself is a molybdenum manganese steel forging; although not initially provided, cross-drillings were added from engine number TS 881E to improve lubrication. The crankshaft rear is sealed with a scroll type oil seal, and at the front within the timing cover a conventional oil seal is used (the scroll type seal is absent on pre-crossdrilled cranks).

A duplex chain drives the camshaft, which in turn drives the distributor and oil pump by skew gears, and also the fuel pump. The camshaft initially had a bearing at the forward end with the three other journals running directly in the block. However, bearings were fitted throughout from engine number TS 8997E. The camshaft drives the eight vertical overhead val-

A view of the other side of the TR3's engine bay, showing the bonnet 'pop-up' spring arrangement mounted behind the centre of the front apron. The dipstick top (painted yellow) and the fan should be black. On the top of the inner wings are the brackets into which the 'Dzus' bonnet fasteners fit when the bonnet is closed.

ves by means of tappets, pushrods and rockers, the inlet valves having double springs and the exhaust valves triple springs. Exhaust valves are 1.3in diameter, inlet valves 1.56in. The cylinder head has eight ports (four inlet and four exhaust), and, looking from the front of the engine, these are on the left-hand side along with the dynamo and starter; the fuel pump, oil filter, distributor and spark plugs are on the right-hand side. Valve timing is relatively conservative at 15°/55°/55°/15°, and valve lift is 0.375in.

Power output for the TR2 in 'low-port' form is 90bhp at 4800rpm, with the maximum torque of 117lb ft occurring at 3000rpm. The safe maximum engine speed was considered to be 5000rpm, although occasional use to 5500rpm appears to do no harm.

Spark plugs were originally specified as Champion L10S, the gap being quoted as .032in. A Lucas DM2 distributor was fitted, and the oil filter was a Purolator 'Micronic' type 17F/5102. This was the initial 'by-pass' filter, but from engine number TS12650E a Purolator full-flow filter system was introduced. The handbook quotes the oil pressure as 'between 40 and 60lb/sq in when car is travelling at normal speeds and the oil is hot'. Oil capacity with the filter from dry is 11 pints.

Other than as detailed above, the basic TR engine was little modified during its long production run, apart from changes to the cylinder head and piston arrangements. These are described in detail in 'Production Changes' at the end of this chapter, but, briefly, four types of head were used. The basic low-port TR2 head was used up to the introduction of the TR3, and then, for a short while, a slightly modified low-port head – with its ports opened out to make best use of the larger 1¾in SU carburettors – was fitted to increase power to 95bhp. At engine number TS 9350E, the 'Le Mans' low-port head became available, combining the best features of the two earlier designs. Finally, phased in somewhat erratically from engine number TS 12606E, came the 'high-port' design, with larger inlet ports set higher in the head contributing to better breathing. The high-port head allowed the engine to develop around 100bhp, giving a marginal improvement in performance. Fuel consumption also rose, and cars equipped with the high-port heads and larger carburettors can never equal the early TR2s for economy. High-port heads required longer cylinder head studs. It was found necessary to beef up the pistons by making them stiffer no fewer than three times, at engine numbers TS 4883E, TS 9731E and TS26698E. The piston ring type and disposition was also changed during these modifications.

Some controversy surrounds the colour in which the engines were painted. The great majority were finished in black, and a 'sidescreeen' car engine painted black could not, I think, be criticised. However, I have seen examples purporting to be original painted in dark blue, in a kind of sea-green metallic finish, and in red. Cylinder heads were usually black, but other colours undoubtedly appeared, principally the sea-green. Ancillaries – dynamo, starter, horns, oil filter, engine mounts, wiper motor, air cleaners and initially the rocker cover – were also black, but I have seen red starter and wiper motors which were claimed as original, and silver-painted air cleaners existed.

The black-painted rocker cover sometimes had the tappet clearances written on it by means of a white transfer, and the oil filler/breather, again painted black, also carried a white transfer specifying the oils to be used (but this sometimes rubbed off in use). At engine number TS 18230, the black

rocker cover gave way to a more stylish chromed one, along with a hammer-finish silver-painted oil filler/breather. The thermostat housing and inlet manifolds should be left as cast.

COOLING SYSTEM

This is a conventional system incorporating a radiator, water pump, by-pass, thermostat and fan. The system is pressurised at 4lb/sq in, and its capacity is 13 pints (or 14 if a heater is fitted).

The workshop manual states that the thermostat begins to open at 70°C, and is fully open at 92°C. The most suitable thermostat for British conditions is that quoted as an '82°C' one. The correct thermostat should incorporate a 'bypass blanking ring' to ensure that the bypass hose route is cut off once the thermostat opens. If this is not done, overheating can develop. Unfortunately, these correct thermostats are now difficult to obtain. Normal running temperature is denoted by the central mark on the temperature gauge as 185°F (85°C), and a cooling system in good condition should have no trouble in keeping down to this temperature.

The water pump bolts directly to the front of the engine, and is driven, like the dynamo, by a substantial 'V' profile belt. The fan, which was balanced, is driven direct from the crankshaft via an extension piece, and also acts as a vibration damper. It has four blades, and is 12½in in diameter. Owners who have substituted an electric fan have sometimes experienced broken crankshafts owing to the loss of this damping effect. Hoses were of usual black rubber and canvas composition, the steel tube forming part of the bottom hose being painted black.

The front apron style on the TR2 and TR3 provided a natural duct which directed air through the radiator very efficiently, but unfortunately the TR3A's full-width grille and front apron lost some of this efficiency, so these later cars are more prone to overheating. To try to address this, the TR3A was fitted with an air deflector inside the grille, but the composition material from which it was made proved not to be very durable. If your TR3A overheats, especially at speed, be sure that it has its air deflector.

Few other modifications were found to be necessary to the cooling system of sidescreen TRs. The principal one was the deletion of the early type 'double-width'

thermostat housing at TS 1201 in favour of the simpler 'single' type. This modification changed the relative position of the radiator top hose outlet, so that pre-TS 1201 radiators differ slightly from all the later ones. All radiators should have a 1½in square hole to allow the starting handle to pass through to the crankshaft dog, but many cars have been fitted with rebuilt (or TR4 type) radiators where this hole has been deleted for simplicity and cheapness. The radiator is bolted at its base to the front chassis cross-tube, and two stays support the top, connecting it to the inner wings with screwed rods which give some adjustment.

The heater was always an optional extra, although it was supplied from new on most UK-delivered cars, and fitted retrospectively on others. Cars sent to hot climates often, not surprisingly, had no heater even where many other 'extras' had been specified. Where fitted, the heater, manufactured by Smiths Industries, sits under the front scuttle behind the dashboard, and acts also as a windscreen demister by means of ducting to two vent nozzles situated just behind the windscreen. The base of the heater has two hinged 'doors', and if both are shut hot air goes to the demisting ducts. Either one or both 'doors' can be opened to direct air to the desired side of the car.

The heater blower motor is rheostatically controlled from a rotary switch on the dashboard, and the amount of hot water reaching the heater can be controlled from under the bonnet by means of a brass tap inserted into the cylinder head. The heater was quoted in the factory literature as having an output of 3½ kilowatts, but this would seem a most optimistic rating!

The radiator, heater unit and water pump were painted black. The fan should be black, although some appear to have been finished in red.

EXHAUST SYSTEM

A cast, unpainted four-branch manifold (originally made by Qualcast Ltd) feeds into a single curved downpipe via a flanged joint with a copper/asbestos gasket. The downpipe passes alongside the engine sump and very close to the inner side of the cruciform chassis bracing. The first mounting point is situated by the gearbox crossmember, and at the same point the downpipe feeds into the centre section of the three-piece system, the mounting doubling

TR3A engine bay in 'show' condition – more highly polished than a standard production car would have been. The engine and water pump should be black, and the wiper motor should not be chromed. Both body numbers are clearly seen on the bulkhead. The flasher unit, washer bottle and the run of the brakepipes above the pedal box are incorrect, while the regulator/control box appears to have been fitted at 90° to the correct position.

as a pipe clamp. This section contains the silencer box, and passes right through the central box member of the chassis cruciform bracing, the silencer box itself being situated aft of the cruciform centre. The section containing the silencer then joins a long tailpipe with a curve in it, to bring the exhaust system – passing under the rear axle – out at the rear of the car on the left-hand side slightly below the overrider.

Early TR2s (up to TS 2531) had only an 18in long silencer box, which by all accounts was extremely noisy even by the standards of the day. Thereafter, until TS 11385, a 24in box was fitted, which improved matters only slightly. From that point, the plain tailpipe section was deleted, and a second, 12in silencer box with a shorter integral tailpipe was added to counter continuing criticisms of noise. This was further modified at TS 15705. Both silencer boxes were of the straight-through pattern. The second and final mounting point was about 9in from the rear of the system, and consisted of a pipe clamp suspended by a strap from a bracket on the cross tube.

The exhaust system diameter was 1⅞in, and as originally supplied, certainly for TR2s, the system was painted black. However, replacements have been silver or aluminium colour painted for many years, and either colour can be considered correct. A chromed tail pipe finisher also existed and was apparently fitted to many early TR2s, but not throughout the production run. The original type fitted *inside* the tailpipe with the chromed piece protruding, but it is believed that there was a later type that fitted externally.

CARBURETTORS & FUEL SYSTEM

In the 1950s, the application of twin (or triple) SU carburettors was almost *de rigueur* for a British engine with sporting pretensions, and the TR series was no exception.

The TR2 had a pair of H4 type 1½in SUs of a semi-downdraught design, mounted on a cast aluminium inlet manifold with a two-stud fixing for each carburettor. Twin air filters of the 'pancake' or drum wire mesh type were fitted, and the carburettors themselves had brass hexagonal dashpot tops, rather than the later black plastic type. The standard needle for the H4 carburettors was type 'FV'; the Driver's Handbook suggested the substitution of type 'GC' for competition or high-speed work.

Fuel was pumped by an AC mechanical fuel pump (type number 'UE') sited on the cylinder block on the opposite side to the carburettors, and driven directly from the camshaft. The pump incorporated a wire mesh filter gauze and a glass sediment bowl. Because the fuel tank was situated in an unusually high position, a brass fuel tap was incorporated into the fuel system, mounted on the chassis frame below the fuel pump. By closing this tap with a push and twist action, the tank could be isolated if the carburettors or fuel pump required dismantling.

The tank, originally of 12½ gallons capacity, is positioned sideways across the car below the rear bulkhead and forward of the boot space. It is filled directly from above, the fuel filler being a chromium, snap-action, quick-release type mounted centrally. The pipework from the tank to the carburettors was predominantly in nickel-plated steel, with brass 'banjo' type connections onto the carburettor float chambers and brass unions. The correct run of the feed pipe is around the front of the cylinder head, where it should be clipped to the lower bolt on the thermostat front outlet housing. The section of pipe from the petrol tap to the fuel pump was in reinforced braided flexible piping, to allow for engine movement; this was modified to a simpler design at TS 15496.

With the introduction of the TR3, larger H6 type 1¾in SU carburettors were introduced, with a four-stud fixing and a suitably modified inlet manifold. These originally had 'TD' needles, which were quickly replaced by 'TE' ones. Neither proved satisfactory, rapid development work resulting in the fitment of the 'SM' needle which continued to be standard during the rest of the run. With the carburettor change, fuel piping was also modified in an effort to cure fracture problems. A flexible pipe now connected the two carburettors, and continued back to meet the original type rigid pipe at a union adjacent to the thermostat housing. Modified air cleaners were introduced, with an offset to allow for the larger carburettor throats. The petrol tank was reduced to 12 gallons to allow a little more room for the newly introduced optional rear seat. Following the retooling of the TR3A body at TS 60001, the tank-to-petrol-tap piping and attachment points were modified to fit the new body shape at the rear.

The petrol tank itself was finished in black, as were its straps. TR2/3/3A air filters have been seen in silver, black or red, and all may be considered original. The brass components were not highly polished and the inlet manifold was left as cast. The carburettor bodies were mildly polished, but not to a mirror finish.

TRANSMISSION

Other than the usual problems of worn synchromesh occasioned by use and age, the sidescreen TR gearbox gave, and still gives, very little trouble. For this reason, few modifications in production proved necessary, although, of course, the 'TCF' series of TR3Bs had the TR4-type all-synchromesh gearbox. The Laycock overdrive units have also proved reliable in use, provided the filter is kept clean and the solenoid is properly adjusted.

The TR gearbox was derived initially from the Standard Vanguard unit, although this had only three speeds. A similar casing was used, and a four speed transmission – without synchromesh on first – was persuaded inside. The gate pattern is the conventional 'H', with reverse to the right and rear. The Vanguard-style column change mechanism was mercifully discarded, and a neat, remote control unit was provided on

the gearbox top cover, endowing the TR with one of the most positive, pleasant and short-throw changes of its day. Gearbox oil capacity was 1½ pints without overdrive, 3½ pints with overdrive.

The overdrive unit was available right from the start of production, although initial take-up was slow; only around 10–15 per cent of TR2s were fitted with overdrive from the factory. Aside from the cost, possibly one reason was that the car was quite high geared for its day in standard form, at roughly 20mph per 1000rpm in top. Torque was such, however, that the engine had no difficulty in pulling overdrive top of almost 25mph per 1000rpm.

The most important change to the gearbox occurred from TS 6266 in May 1955, when the old overdrive unit, which acted only on top gear, gave way to a new unit acting on second and third gears as well, endowing the car with seven forward speeds. As far as I know, this was unique in 1955 and is still an impressive feature today. By TS 6280 all cars had the 'three overdrive speeds' unit, which necessitated a new gearbox top cover incorporating two isolator switches in lieu of the previous single switch, and modified selectors to operate these switches. As a preparation to the incorporation of overdrive on second and third, uprated overdrive clutch operating pistons were fitted to all cars from TS 5980, and to a few cars prior to this. Piston diameter was increased from 1⅛in to 1⅜in, the new unit being coded 22/1374 (the old one was coded 22/1275). The factory supplied a 'top cover conversion pack' to allow three overdrive speeds to be incorporated on pre TS 6266 gearboxes, although if the smaller pistons were fitted the resulting unit could be marginal under full torque. Starting at TS 26825 and being phased in gradually, gearboxes incorporated needle roller rather than plain bearings in the mainshaft and constant pinion shaft.

The gearbox casing was redesigned for cars after TS 50001 to allow for the new type of starter motor, in which the pinion threw towards the front of the car rather than the reverse as previously; the starter ring gear was consequently modified, with the chamfer on the teeth being cut from the other side. At the same time, the dipstick in the gearbox top cover was replaced by an oil level plug.

Gearbox ratios did not change during the run, but the 4.1:1 final drive became available as an option on overdrive-equipped cars from the introduction of the TR3. The

internal and overall gear ratios were as follows:

	INTERNAL RATIOS	OVERALL RATIOS
First	3.38	12.5
Second	2.00	7.4
Second o/d	1.64	6.07
Third	1.325	4.9
Third o/d	1.086	4.02
Top	1.00	3.7
Top o/d	0.82	3.03
Reverse	4.28	

The appropriate road speeds per 1000rpm, based on the above ratios and on the original fitment of 5.50 × 15 crossply tyres, were: first, 6.00mph; second, 10.1mph; second o/d, 12.3mph; third, 15.2mph; third o/d, 18.5mph; top, 20.2mph; top o/d, 24.6mph. At 100mph, allowing for tyre growth, the engine turned at 4800rpm in ordinary top, and 3900rpm in overdrive top. The 4.1:1 axle reduced these speeds by approximately 10 per cent, giving roughly 22mph per 1000rpm in overdrive top.

Up to TS 2876, the gear lever was a solid two-piece item, the top piece incorporating a non-removeable knob. From TS 2877, a one-piece lever was used, with a removeable knob held in place by a chromed locknut. A new lever incorporating an anti-rattle spring and plunger came in at TS 9593, the later gear levers being hollow. It is thought that this was to allow the overdrive wiring to pass up inside the lever to a switch in the gearknob, a modification that did not reach production. The lever was chromium plated, with a moulded black rubber gaiter at its base which was always prone to splitting. Around the gear lever gaiter hole, the transmission tunnel carpet should have a bound edge, except on early TR2s. The correct gear knob is somewhat pear-shaped and made of hard moulded rubber, although later ones were of plastic. Original knobs are rare, most having been replaced over the years. Several different anti-rattle spring arrangements were tried over the years, but none was wholly satisfactory in curing a buzzing sound in the lever under hard acceleration. The clutch was a hydraulically operated Borg & Beck 9in single dry-plate type.

Gearbox casings were either finished in silver/aluminium paint or left as cast, whereas propshafts were black. The propshaft, by Hardy-Spicer, had universal joints at both ends and a sliding spline at the front to allow for axle movement. The propshaft remained the same whether or not overdrive was fitted, the non-overdrive gearbox having a long tailshaft section to compensate for the missing overdrive unit. The gearbox crossmember was also the same in both applications, and was again painted black. Gearboxes were individually numbered in a separate 'TS' series that roughly equated to the car's commission number.

ELECTRICAL EQUIPMENT & LAMPS

As was usual in the 1950s, Lucas supplied the electrical items. A single 12-volt battery was always used, sited in a battery tray in the centre of the inner front bulkhead, just aft of the cylinder head, and clamped across its outer face by a right angled bar (painted black) with a 'hockey-stick' screwed rod clamp at either end. The battery was initially of 43 AH capacity (ampere hours) with seven plates, but this was later uprated to a nine-plate type of 58 AH. No master switch was fitted, and the wiring loom was of conventional colour coded type, with a cotton covering up to TS 64560. Following that, from December 1959, a plastic-coated loom with snap-on connectors was fitted.

The dynamo and its bracketry were finished in black, and it was driven by 'V' belt from the crankshaft pulley. The type was Lucas C39 PV/2, early examples having a removeable cover band over the brushes, deleted from TS 9843. In 1960 the dynamo type changed to Lucas C40, which had push-on connectors rather than the previous nuts and bolts. The regulator was also mounted on the front bulkhead along with the fuse carrier, which had only two fuses – one of 50 amps, the other 35 amps. Two spare fuses, one of each type, were sited in the fuse carrier. The Lucas regulator and cut-out was of type RB106/1. The ignition coil was of type B12 (later type HA12), usually painted black and attached directly to the cylinder block. The distributor was of the Lucas DM2 pattern, type P4, the contact breaker set initially having two locking screws. Automatic advance and retard by vacuum and weights was fitted. A modified contact set, of the 'pre-fitted' type, was fitted during 1955 at TS 8213, and this type has only one locking screw. Very late TR3As and TR3Bs had Lucas type 25D4

This is the P700 headlight, with 'tripod' bars and hooded bulb. While the P700 is correct for cars from 1955, 1954 cars usually had the plain, non-tripod, F700 type when built. Note the thin wing piping in body colour, one of three different types correct for TR2s.

The early (pre TS 1307) TR2 rear light unit has a separate reflector 'hung-on' by means of a metal strap painted body colour. The rear wings had to be slightly reprofiled when this unit was superseded, as the early light's chrome bezel was a slightly different shape.

distributors. The original type sparking plugs were Champion L10S of ½in reach, but the handbook suggested type L11S for high-speed work and type L10 for low-octane fuel countries. The gap was .032in (0.8mm). Right-angled rubberised plug caps (later plastic) were fitted and the high tension leads were black.

Sidescreen TR starter motors fall into two distinct types: the 'outboard drive' type fitted up to TS 50001, and the 'inboard drive' type used thereafter. These are colloquially known to TR enthusiasts as the 'long' and 'short' starters respectively. Both were activated by a solenoid sited on the

The original Lucas '525' combined central stop and tail light, which also served as number plate illumination. The chromed fixing screws are correct. This unit was fitted to all TR2s, and to all TR3s but a few of the very last ones.

front bulkhead under the bonnet, below the regulator box, the solenoid being energised by a starter button on the dashboard. The earlier motor was Lucas type M418G, the later type being similarly numbered despite its considerable differences! Most starters were painted black, but I have seen red ones claimed as original.

Windscreen wiper blades were usually 8in 'Trico' items, although 8½in or 9in blades are sometimes fitted when the 8in ones are unobtainable. The longer blades, however, can interfere with the hood overlap at the top of the windscreen. The wiper arms and bezels surrounding the wiper spindles were usually chromed. Some early TR2s, however, had bezels in body colour with matt black arms. The Lucas type CRT15 wiper motor was mounted on a bracket on the left-hand side of the front bulkhead under the bonnet, looking from the front. The motor changed to type DR2 (with a self-parking arrangement) at TS 12567 and was repositioned on the other side of the bulkhead. A two-speed wiper motor (originally type DR1) was available as an optional extra. Wipers normally parked on the right on RHD cars and the left on LHD cars.

Twin Lucas 'windtone' horns of considerable power were fitted, the Parts Book indicating that special 'High Frequency' horns were fitted for export markets. The horns were painted black, and mounted either side of the radiator just under the top of the front apron. The original type was WT 614, soon replaced by WT 618; these two types have different trumpet flares. The horns were fitted in matched pairs, one

high-note and one low-note, with the appropriate letter 'H' or 'L' stamped inside the trumpet flares.

Headlamps were by Lucas, of the pre-focus, double-dip type, serial number F700, with block-type lenses. Wattage was 60/36, and the lights initially did not have the well-known 'tripod' bars. Type P700, which did have the tripod arrangement, became available in the UK in 1955 as an option, becoming standard fitment in 1956, although export markets still had the old F700 units. There were also minor variations to suit left- and right-hand dipping, and local regulations in export markets. It is believed that sealed beam units were originally fitted on the TR3A/B for some markets, principally the USA, to comply with regulations. The dipswitch was foot operated. Chromed front rims were fitted to the headlights in addition to the chrome-edged inner rims, with black neoprene type gaskets and dust excluders interposed between the body and the light units.

Sidelamp units, which incorporated flashing direction indicators from the start, were mounted below the headlights, these being Lucas type 488 in either clear or white frosted, diffused glass. From the TR3A, however, different style sidelights were mounted in the grille. The bulbs projected further forward, requiring a more bulbous lens of Lucas type 594. A standard Lucas type FL2 flasher unit was used at first, then uprated to type FL3 from TS 9894, and eventually to type FL5.

Rear lamps were of two distinct types. Early TR2s, up to TS 1300, had Lucas type 471 units, which had lenses with 'squared off' corners, the reflectors being hung separately below the light unit. These units incorporated twin filament bulbs, and doubled as flashing indicators. The chromed bezel was different from that used on cars after TS 1300. Number plate illumination and the stop lamp function were combined in a Lucas 525 unit mounted centrally on the rear apron above the spare wheel door. Cars after TS 1300 had Lucas rear lights of type 549, which had plastic lenses with a built-in reflector; these continued to be employed throughout the production run. Again, these lights incorporated the flashing indicators at first, the central stop lamp still being used. However, regulations in certain export markets – notably USA, Holland and Belgium – began to dictate the use of twin stop lamps and/or separate flashing indicators, so these were incorporated towards the end of TR3 production, in a

The reversing light is a period accessory, and the chromed tail-pipe finisher was fitted to most early TR2s. Note the correct teardrop-shaped escutcheons covering the boot 'budget' locks, and the central key lock. The neat, original, matching hood-stick cover is as it should be, but the rear orange indicators and screen-mounted mirror are additions. Note also the body-coloured wing piping along the wings to body joins. The number plate is mounted on the spare wheel trap-door.

somewhat *ad hoc* manner. One cannot be definite as to exactly when separate flashers (Lucas type 594 again, with orange lenses) and a central 'number plate only' light came in and for which markets, nor as to whether the mounting-plinth pressings for the separate flashers were incorporated in the rear apron at the same time – although probably they were. By the end of TR3 production in September 1957, all cars, even home market ones, certainly had these modifications, but the parts books do not record the change point. TR3As and TR3Bs continued with the same arrangement, the new chromed number plate lamp being Lucas type 467-2.

BODY & BODY TRIM

Steel body panels were used almost entirely, the only exceptions being the aluminium bonnet and spare wheel door on very early TR2s. The body steelwork was in either 19 or 20swg (.042 to 035in). The job of assembly was contracted out to Mulliners after the first few TR2s were built by

Standard-Triumph. TR3B bodies, incidentally, were built by the Forward Radiator Company.

Repair and restoration is eased by the fact that many TR panels were bolted rather than welded, something that home mechanics have long had cause to be grateful for. The outer wings and front apron panel were bolted in place; even the inner sills were bolted to the chassis outriggers, although welding was also involved. In contrast to MGAs and Austin-Healeys, the entire body, including bulkheads, can be lifted complete from the chassis once the mounting bolts are undone and other disconnections made. However, there is a risk that a body weakened by rust will collapse about the door apertures if this is attempted.

The central core of the body is formed by the front bulkhead and separate scuttle assembly, front inner wings, floors either side, inner sills (and outer sills on short-doored cars), inner and outer quarter panels, 'A' and 'B' posts, rear floor and propshaft cover section, rear inner wings, boot floor, rear apron and rear tonneau panel assembly. These items are welded to

This very late TR3 has been fitted from new with separate amber rear flashers and the TR3A type number plate lamp. The boot rack is of the original chromed 'swinging' type, the forward mounts of which are attached to the boot hinges. On the TR3, the body-coloured wing bead gave way to the stainless steel type shown here. The later TR2 and TR3/3A 'Reflex' rear light units are also seen.

Separate amber rear flashers and a chromed number plate light were standard on the homemarket TR3A, although red rear flashers were fitted for some export markets. Note also the external boot handle (the boot 'budget' locks were deleted) and the maker's name badge, added for the first time on the TR3A.

form a cohesive unit onto which the bolted panels are fixed, along with ancillary items such as the spare wheel pan, rear rail and body mounting brackets. As mentioned in the 'Production Changes' section, bodies made after commission number TS 60001 differ considerably around the rear floor panel and elsewhere, but, in principle, the same basic body construction and panels were used throughout.

Doors originally had no external handles on TR2s and TR3s, although the installation of the 'Grand Touring' hardtop kit would have occasioned their fitting. Internal pull cords operated TR2 and TR3 doors. TR3As and Bs had external handles, and cars after TS 60001 had doors with dif-

ferent shaped bottoms to their internal framework. An interior pull was still incorporated on all TR3As, but moved to inside the door pocket.

Each door on all models had two hinges – brass up to body number EB 54335, thereafter steel – and a steel checkstrap stay. Wooden members were incorporated internally in the doors near their tops, to allow for fine tuning of the position of the two sidescreen sockets on each door, these being screwed to the wooden pieces. Chromed pockets were fitted up to TS 28825; these received the wedge-shaped ends of the sidescreen locating arms which were clamped in place by knurled thumbscrews. From TS 28826, a different sidescreen

fixing was employed using a flat socket with a Dzus ¼-turn fastener operated by the bonnet lock carriage key. The door apertures were weather-sealed by rubber piping covered in vynide material to match the trim colour, and a black rubber sealing strip at the top forward end of the door under the front bulkhead. An aluminium kick plate ran along the inside and top of the inner sill, and the door had a rubber sealing strip that closed onto the sill to exclude water. TR3A/Bs had Furflex piping rather than the Vynide covered type.

The bonnet was hinged at the rear with two external hinges, painted body colour on TR2s and chromed subsequently. Up to TS 4228, a complex, twin-lock, internal re-

A period type of wing mirror, correct for a TR2. Also seen is the chromed 'Dzus', ¼-turn button for securing the bonnet; two of these replaced the earlier internal bonnet locks in October 1954.

Boot (and bonnet) hinges on TR2s should be painted body colour. They are 'handed' left and right. The small 'pip' acted as a stop should the hinge go 'over-centre' and threaten to break.

Two TR3A views showing the spare wheel door opened (revealing the correct rubber seal) and closed. The two painted metal tongues at either side of the compartment are for engaging with the tongues on the ¼-turn budget locks that keep the door in place. The spare wheel strap and tool strap are correct, although reproduction items. The tool strap on the right-hand side holds the jack and handle. The 'Triumph' badge is a one-piece item, unlike the individual letters on the front apron.

lease bonnet latch mechanism was used, but from TS 4229, a simple ¼-turn Dzus fastening system operated by the carriage key 'T-bar' was employed, principally to save cost. Early bonnets had four air outlets at their trailing edge but later ones had only two. The trailing edge of some bonnets was also flanged to ensure that paint adhered more easily. However, this made it impossible to grind the edge to perfect the fit, so it was rapidly discontinued. Unfortunately, it cannot be established exactly when these changes occurred.

Bodies after TS 60001 had the bonnet (and boot) hinges raised slightly on plinths formed in the bulkheads and the relevant panels. All bonnets had a safety catch mechanism at their forward edge, and 'Dzus fastener' bonnets had a 'spring and pillar' type of mechanism to raise the bonnet sufficiently to allow a finger to be inserted to operate the release. The bonnet had to be propped open manually; the body coloured prop was situated on the right-hand side and located into a plate forming part of the safety catch mechanism. On all sidescreen cars two adjustable posts with rubber buffers, one each side, served to locate the forward edge of the bonnet when closed. The chromed Dzus fasteners were retained in the bonnet by push-fit washers.

External hinges were also fitted to the boot, and again painted body colour on the TR2 and chromed on later cars. Bonnet and boot hinges were made of Mazak and are prone to fracture if strained unduly. A body colour boot stay was fitted, pivoting from the bootlid and engaging in an elongated slot on the right-hand side of the boot aperture. Originally no key-operated locks were intended to be fitted to the TR2, boot locking being achieved by two 'budget' locks, one on each side of the lid, operated by the 'T-bar' carriage key. These budget locks were covered by hinged, chromed escutcheons, which were teardrop shaped initially and later circular. However, by the time production began, a central key lock was also fitted to the boot lid, providing three separate means of locking! The key was the same as the ignition key, unlike that

The correct position for the TR2's front number plate is as shown; also visible is the narrow (10½in) spacing of the windscreen wiper spindles, but the wiper blades are incorrect on this car. (Spacing was increased to 14½in in March 1954). The spotlights and badge bar are correct for the period, but the large mirror is an addition. Grilles were either chromed Mazak or die-cast buffed aluminium. Note also the correct type of sidelights with frosted glass lenses.

This view shows the chromed 'reveal' moulding fitted round the 'mouth' of later TR2s. Unlike the TR3 type, it does not continue across the top of the aperture. Two nice additional lamps of the period are shown, but the cork fitted in the starting handle guide is not standard! The badge bar, sidelight and overrider are correct.

for the glove box lid on early cars. This arrangement continued until the TR3A, when a separate, external, key-lockable boot handle was fitted centrally and the budget locks were deleted. The boot had a moulded rubber weather seal let into a channel all around the opening, and two drain tubes, one in each bottom corner, collected water from the boot area and ensured (if not blocked) that it passed harmlessly out into the rear wheel arch area via holes in the boot side panels, through which the drain tubes passed.

The spare wheel inhabited a very practical compartment in the tail. Access was gained via a trapdoor on which the number plate was mounted. This door was retained by two more 'Budget' locks, again covered with circular, chromed, spring-loaded es-

cutcheons operated by the 'T-bar'. The spare wheel was retained by a leather strap, eye and buckle arrangement, with a second strap, eye and buckle for the jack and tools.

Two different types of chromed front bumper blade were fitted. The TR2/3 type was mounted on four irons, two at each side, which bolted to the front chassis legs. Overriders were fitted, with black piping between them and the bumper blade. The front number plate was invariably attached to the bumper direct, rather than mounted below it. TR3A/B bumpers differed considerably, with a more bulbously rounded cross-section. Although they were still attached to the chassis legs by bumper irons, additional supports ran from the overriders through the grille to mount on the inner front wings, as further defence against

American parking habits.

No full bumper was fitted at the rear – just a pair of upright chromed overriders either side of the spare wheel door. Each overrider was bolted to the chassis at the base by means of a strong bracket on to the rear chassis rails, and near the top via an angled bolt and tube arrangement which passed through the rear apron to bolt onto the rear chassis rails. Bumper irons and fixings should be painted black. The rear number plate was fixed directly to a raised pressing in the spare wheel door.

Three distinct types of front grille were fitted. Within the TR2's front apron 'mouth', a chromed Mazak grille was inserted just in front of the radiator, the ¾in square sections of this grille giving some protection to the radiator from flying stones. On some cars this grille was made from die-cast, buffed aluminium rather than chromed Mazak. The TR2's mouth originally had steelwork continuing all round the aperture internally, whereas the TR3 type had cutaways at the top, presumably to reduce airflow through the radiator and to increase it into the engine compartment generally. Since this difference is not apparent in a normal view of the car, one has to look up into the mouth aperture from bumper level to spot it.

One of the unsolved mysteries of sidescreen TRs is exactly when the chromium 'reveal' moulding was fitted around the mouth aperture on TR2s. Exhaustive study of the works literature has

The TR3 'eggbox' cellular grille was made of polished aluminium; the chrome 'reveal' moulding is separate from the grille, and carries on all around the aperture. The domed glasses on the sidelight units are correct for a late TR3 with separate rear flashers; the P700 headlight is also correct.

failed to establish this, but certainly most, if not all, later TR2s had this feature. The moulding did not continue across the top of the mouth aperture, unlike the TR3 type which ran all the way round the mouth. A chromed starting handle guide was fitted to the front apron and anchored at its base to the foremost chassis crosstube. The starting handle passed through the grille and right through the radiator to engage with the crankshaft nose extension piece.

The TR3 had what has become known as the 'cellular' or 'eggbox' grille. This polished aluminium grille screwed into place in the front apron in an attempt to update the car's styling. A chromed 'reveal' moulding continuing all around the mouth was also fitted. The TR3A and B, of course, have a completely different grille and front apron, the latter having the headlight pods further back. The full width grille is again of polished aluminium and has the sidelight/flashers mounted within it. As previously, the starting handle passes through the grille and a guide before reaching the crankshaft. Fixed by self-tapping screws around its edge, the TR3A grille can be easily removed for maintenance.

There is very little ornamentation on the TR2/3/3A/3B, almost every fitting being functional. The leading edge of the rear wings has a polished, pressed aluminium stoneguard clipped around the wing and pinched in place between the wing and the quarter panel. Forward of this is one of the few non-functional items, the stoneguard

'foot' which adorns the bottom of the quarterpanel. Again, this is a polished aluminium pressing.

Beading was always fitted between the wings and the main section of the body. This was made in stainless steel on TR3s, 3As and 3Bs, and held in place by adjustable tabs that were pinched as the wings were bolted up. On TR2s, however, the beading was in body colour material, usually a kind of Vynide fabric and rubber piping concoction. There were certainly two, and possibly three, different types of this beading, the variation being in the cross-section and material type. Some TR2 beading had a string type centre covered in Vynide. Information is scant on this subject and the beading itself is very hard to find today, causing many problems for those restoring TR2s to

The front view of the TR3A shows the correct headlamps, and the new grille and bumper. The 'Triumph' medallion is now enamelled in blue and white rather than the previous red and black. The 'Triumph' lettering is the earlier 'ribbed' type; the later 'smooth' type was introduced at TS 60001.

The Triumph medallion was used in various forms on all TRs from 1953 to the end of the TR4 production in 1965. A little-known fact is that the base of the 'U' in the word Triumph was fractionally higher than the base of the other letters – optical illusion would otherwise have caused it to look too low.

The 'TR3' bonnet medallion, with a rare and original matching key fob.

board of these, in turn, is the screen frame itself, formed of chrome on brass; the glass, usually laminated, sits on a bedding of rubber. These separate parts were screwed together by three chromed brass set screws at each side. If replacement screws are used, incidentally, they must be of the correct length; if too long, they can crack the screen glass when tightened. The screen top rail has a black rubber seal to seal against the hood, and 10 Tenax fastening pegs for the hood are screwed into the screen top rail, facing forwards. The bottom seal is again a black rubber moulding which slides into an appropriate groove at the base of the screen frame. Some later TR3As (post 60001) had cast aluminium rather than chromed screen frames and stanchions – but no change point has been found and it is thought that few were produced.

Inner wings, the under bonnet and boot area, wheel arches, floors and bulkheads were all painted body colour. In fact, it is believed that all parts of the body as constructed by Mulliners were body coloured, although it usually pays not to be categorical in these matters. The main dimensions of the complete car were as follows:

full originality. Unlike later cars, where the stainless steel beading ran alongside the bonnet aperture, on TR2s the beading stopped where the front apron met the bonnet, and resumed for a short run at the front scuttle/wing joint. The parts book lists the required beading lengths for TR2s: rear wing front portion, 68½in; rear portion (below the rear lights), 10⅛in; front wing, 27½in; front scuttle, 9⁵⁄₁₆in. TR2 beading was supplied by the foot, while TR3/3A/3B beading came preformed in correct lengths.

Badging on the TR2 and 3 was minimal. The only identification was provided by a medallion fixed to the centre of the front apron. This shield, a combination of red and black vitreous enamel and chrome, included the word 'Triumph' and 'TR2' or 'TR3' as appropriate. There was no identification at the rear of the car. On the TR3A, the front medallion continued, red and black at first, but changed to blue and white at TS 41878. However, the word 'Triumph' was deleted from the medallion on TR3As because separate chromed Mazak letters spelling the manufacturer's name were fitted on the front apron below the medallion. There were two types of these individual letters, one type dished and ridged and the other type plain, the latter utilised from body number EB72384.

Lack of rear identification was rectified on the TR3A/B by fitting to the rear apron (just below the boot opening) a one-piece 'Triumph' badge with the name underlined. Again this was a chromed Mazak item and prone to breakage. On cars for certain markets, notably the USA, it is believed that additional 'TR3' badges were sometimes fitted at the rear.

The windscreen was of the 'quick-re-

lease' type with two spring-loaded Dzus ¼-turn screws on each side. Once these were undone and the wipers removed or folded forward, the screen itself could be slid forward on its locating plates and then removed entirely – perhaps a 30sec operation. The locating plates were fixed to the scuttle sides by set screws. For some reason, the post TS 60001 cars with retooled bodies had bolts, rather than quick release fasteners, to locate the screen.

The screen assembly itself is both heavy and surprisingly complex. At each side, a chromed stanchion forms the main member. Inboard of these are chromed tenon plates, which project backwards slightly beyond the stanchion in the hope of providing a seal with the sidescreen. In-

Overall length	12ft 7in	3.84m
Overall width	4ft 7½in	1.41m
Height (hood up)	4ft 2½in	1.28m
Height of scuttle	3ft 4in	1.02m
Wheelbase	7ft 4in	2.24m
Front track	3ft 9in	1.14m
Rear track	3ft 9½in	1.16m
Min. ground clearance	6in	15.2cm
Dry shipping weight	1981lb	902kg
Kerb weight	2107lb	955kg

NB: Weight figures apply to the TR2; later cars were slightly heavier.

A nicely original pair of TR3 seats with contrasting piping. This trim colour is believed to be the rare Vermillion. The gear lever knob is incorrect and the carpets have been replaced; the gearbox tunnel carpet would originally have been made in three pieces with a rubber plug for gearbox level inspection incorporated. The later, fatter, chromed passenger grab handle is seen, and the tonneau/sidescreen fastenings are now 'lift-a-dot' types.

This TR2 has original leather seat facings, in faded Geranium with matching piping. Note the correct wheel arch trimming arrangements, but the carpet on this car is not original. At the top of the windscreen can be seen a correct hard top fixing which must have been retro-fitted to this early car. The correct type of gear lever knob can be seen, as can the earlier type of thin, black-covered grab handle. The ashtray, just visible under the dashboard, is of the incorrect long pull-out type rather than the swivel-out type.

INTERIOR TRIM, BOOT & HOOD

Two distinct types of bucket seats were fitted to these cars. The early type, fitted to TR2s and TR3s, had fixed backrests of thin wrap-around section, the steel of the backrest and seat pan being built-up into one solid section. A separate seat cushion, upholstered in traditional manner with 'Laleweb' springs and horsehair, dropped into the seat pan. The backrest was upholstered and padded, but not very substantially. Some foam rubber padding was used later in the production run, but the change point is uncertain.

On the TR2/3 seats the upholstery 'panelling' of cushions and backrests ran 'front to back', whereas on TR3A seats it ran transversely. The edges of panelled areas and the extremities of the seats themselves always had piping: on TR2s piping usually matched the seat colour, whereas on many TR3s and TR3As it was contrasting. Vynide was always the standard trim material, with leather as an option. Almost all the very early cars had leather specified, with the following trim pieces in this material: cushion and squab main panels and central pleated panels; front bulkhead trim rail; door top rails; quarter pillars; door pulls. Remaining trim items, including the backs of the seats, were in Vynide, even on 'leather' cars. However, a note in the factory records indicates that Rexine was used to trim the carpet welting and scuttle side strips on all cars.

Mention needs to be made of the so-called 'Metric' trim fitted to a few late TR2s and early TR3s. This was a Vynide type material with a curious cross-hatched pattern in relief. On the one such car I have seen, the overall effect was not particularly pleasing. It is unknown how many cars were so fitted, for how long it was available, and if it could be specified or 'just came' whether or not the buyer required it. Certainly it was not in the options list, nor is it referred to in the parts books or manuals – but cars thus trimmed were definitely built.

The seats could move on sliding adjusters, but it appears that an unknown number of early cars were built with a non-adjustable passenger seat. With the advent of the TR3's optional occasional rear seat, the

This interior view shows the TR3A type occasional rear seat – this is the later, post TS 60001 type, with more right-angled front corners. These TR3A type seats are quite different from the TR3 style item. The map light on the dashboard is an accessory of the correct period.

The boot carpet on TR3As was Hardura, black millboard being used for the boot front panel. The flange on the millboard shown here is incorrect. The water drain holes, which must be kept clear, can just be seen in the channel at the bottom of the boot. The tool kit is substantially correct, but is a

reproduction rather than original item. Note the tongue on the inner rear edge of the boot aperture fitted to engage with the new external-handle boot lock.

passenger's side backrest was made to pivot forward to allow easier access to the rear. This occasional rear seat, trimmed like the main seats, was a one-piece item with two brackets forming legs that could be bolted to the floor. The TR3A type, on the other hand, had no built-in backrest: the backrest was formed by pleated Vynide with padding being added to the millboard panel in front of the petrol tank, and a separate cushion. Again, this seat had legs which bolted to the floor.

TR3A bucket seats had thicker backrests with more substantial padding than the earlier seats, and the cushions also benefitted from more padding.

Carpets, stated to be of 'quality 1185', were supplied by the firm of T. F. Firth. The floors, rear floor and heel boards, propshaft and gearbox tunnels, lower front bulkhead, footwell sides, footwells and boot floor were all carpeted. The edges were stitched and bound with Rexine or Vynide. TR3As had boot mats in Hardura, whereas on the TR2/3, Karvel was used. This did not fray, and thus needed no edging. Press studs fixed the carpet to the floors, but carpet on the bulkheads and footwell sides was glued. The side piece carpet in the footwell on the driver's side contained a semi-circular rubber protection pad to avoid wear caused by the action of the side of the foot on the accelerator. Underfelt was not normally fitted. The Parts Catalogues imply that rubber mats rather than carpets were fitted in the footwells

from TS 5089 onwards, but it is not clear whether at that time carpeting was still fitted underneath, or whether the rubber mats replaced the footwell carpet. Certainly by the time the TR3A was introduced, footwell rubber mats were standard and no footwell carpet was provided.

Vynide-covered millboard was used for the boot front (behind the petrol tank) and the quarter panels and rear bulkhead/petrol tank area inside the cockpit, although on TR3As this latter was padded and pleated, even if no occasional seat cushion was fitted. Padded Vynide was stuck onto the wheel arches, with a line of piping following the radius of the arch. The wheel arches in the boot, the boot sides and rear were untrimmed and painted body colour.

Board covered in Vynide was used for the door trims, which were screwed in place with self-tapping screws and held by the sidescreen sockets. Vynide-trimmed pockets were formed in both doors and made in a heavy cardboard composition material. Early TR2s had pockets with corners that that were more right-angled than those of the later pockets. On TR2/3s with no external handles, door latch pulls were fitted. These were Vynide or leather covered wires running from the forward sidescreen pocket to the chrome-headed bolt that operates the lock striker mechanism. On TR3A/Bs, the door pulls were mounted inside the door pockets, and ran inside the doors; they were black plastic covered wire of Bowden cable type.

This is an original 'Stanpart' geranium hood, fitted with the small 'Tenax' fasteners. However, this hood has the post October 1954 three-piece backlight, which would not be original to this early TR2; the hood should have a smaller single rear window. Note the correct cockpit capping rails trimmed to match the upholstery.

Padded trim rolls were fixed by self-tapping screws to the door tops and made of Vynide (or leather) covered foam padding on an aluminium base. Similar, but unpadded, trim rails continued around the top of the sides and rear of the cockpit, all these items being trimmed to match the basic upholstery colour. On the TR3A, chromed finisher buttons were fitted at each end of the door trim.

Hoodsticks were permanently attached to the car, folding neatly across the rear of the cockpit just below its top. These were secured to the body by two large flat-headed set screws each side. The correct spacing of the sticks when erected – which is critical to a properly fitting hood – is provided by two bands of webbing (black or fawn) attached to the rear cockpit rail on each side by a small screwed plate. Each band is attached to each of the three hoodstick bows by self-tapping screws and small plates. Hoodsticks were usually black or red, although silver painted hoodsticks are found and claimed as original. A neat cover for the hoodsticks was normally supplied in the same colour as the hood and sidescreens, although this was often deleted if the optional full tonneau cover was ordered. The hoodstick cover was secured on the Tenax buttons used for the hood's rear fixing, and at the front tucked under the folded hoodsticks.

Two main types of hood were fitted. Cars up to TS 4306 had hoods with only a central rear window, of smaller area than

the later window. Because of restricted visibility, from TS 4307 a three-piece window hood was supplied, with an extra triangular window at each rear corner. Original hoods were made from Vynide-covered canvas and hood windows were in Bakelite Ltd's 'Vybak' of .040in gauge (type number VB215). Hoods and sidescreens matched in colour – full details are in the 'Colours' section.

Tenax buttons and posts were initially used to fix the hood at front and rear, and originally small-headed Tenax buttons were used. From TS 3514, stronger, larger Tenax fasteners were employed. While Tenax fixings were always used to fasten the front of the hood to the windscreen rail, the rear hood fastenings on later cars could be the 'Lift-a-dot' type. One cannot be

This picture shows the early TR2 door pockets with squarer corners than those used later. The chromed sidescreen sockets and trimmed door pull are also clearly seen, as is the interior of a 'long' door, showing the flange at the base. The correct 'Furflex' trim running from the scuttle down the 'A' post can be seen, as can the aluminium sill finisher running along the sill top.

This view shows the early type sidescreen, with a non-sliding 'Vybak' window and a zip fastener to gain access to the internal door release. The 'lift-a-dot' fasteners on the hood of this TR2 are incorrect for its age (Bill Piggott photo).

This 'short door' TR2 side view clearly shows the outer sill, introduced below the shortened doors in October 1954. Also seen is the later sidescreen with the 'Vybak' panes and no zip fastener. The rear pane slides forward to allow access and ventilation. The lower part of the sidescreen still hinges upwards once the fasteners have been undone.

A TR3 newly re-imported from the USA shows the tonneau cover fitted, and also the original 48-spoke painted wire wheels, still carrying white-wall crossply tyres. The brake drum should be black. The perspex wind deflectors were commonly fitted in the USA as an accessory (Bill Piggott photo).

This TR3A view shows the later type 'Dzus' fixing sidescreen, without the hinged bottom. The bottom of the sidescreen does not pick up on the tonneau fixings but ends slightly above them – unlike the earlier type of sidescreen. The polished alloy stoneguard and stoneguard 'foot' are clearly seen. The two rivets on the sidescreen hold a fixing strap on the inside.

categorical that either type is right or wrong for a particular car or period. 'Lift-a-dot' fixings were also usually used to fasten the base of the earlier type of sidescreens to the tops of the doors, but again the Tenax type appeared as well, particularly on early TR2s.

Sidescreen designs and change points are dealt with in detail in the 'Production Changes' section, but here is a summary. TR2s up to TS 5254 had fixed windows of flexible 'Vybak' with hinged signalling flap bottoms, zips being incorporated for access to the interior door pulls. Hardtop-equipped TR2s had sidescreens with sliding perspex rear side windows, the forward part of the side window still being of flexible Vybak. Zips were deleted on these, as interior access was gained by sliding the window. These sliding type sidescreens were brought in for all TRs from TS 5255 onwards, but the hinged flap was still incorporated and the fixings to the doors remained the 'wedge' socket type. From TS 28826, the later Dzus fastening sidescreens became standard. These had a fixed Vynide panel without hinges below the windows, so there were no longer direct fixings to the door by outside fasteners. The full tonneau cover was listed as an extra, although it was usually supplied. Like the hood, the matching tonneau was made from Vynide-covered canvas with a central zip fastener. It picked up on the same rear fastenings as the hood, and on side fixings along the tops of the doors and behind them. Again, these

fastenings could be either Tenax or Lift-a-dot. Finally, a row of eight fastenings, usually Lift-a-dot (but Tenax were used on early cars), was fitted on the front scuttle just behind the windscreen. The usual tonneau pocket, positioned for left- or right-hand drive, was incorporated to allow for the steering wheel. Some tonneaux are seen with additional 6in zips running vertically just aft of the doors to allow for easier folding – it seems that these could be original features.

DASHBOARD & INSTRUMENTS

On TR2s and TR3s, the dashboard was a steel pressing with a separate removeable central section, the whole trimmed to match the colour of the interior trim of the

A clear view of the post TS 28825 sidescreen fixings, these being 'Dzus' ¼-turn fasteners operated by a carriage key, giving a more positive location than the earlier wedge type. The strap on the lower inside of the sidescreen should be attached to a press-stud on the door.

The instrumentation and switchgear are correct on this TR3, with the exception of the flick switch where the 'barrel' overdrive switch (if fitted) would normally go on the extreme right. The correct type of handbrake grip and one of the TR3/ 3A type chromed bonnet hinges are also visible.

car. A glovebox was incorporated on the passenger's side, the lid similarly trimmed. A modest alteration for the TR3A was that the central section carrying the minor instruments was given a black crackle finish, in contrast to the remainder of the fascia. The glovebox was lockable and its interior was formed of a composition board that could disintegrate due to water ingress. The key was originally different to the ignition key, but later the same key was used. An aluminium capping trim rail covered in trim fabric, bending down at either side, was fitted along the front bulkhead above the dashboard.

One of the joys of a sidescreen TR is the splendidly impressive and comprehensive set of instruments, all but one manufactured by Jaeger, a division of Smiths Industries Ltd. In front of the driver are a large matching speedometer and rev counter. Convex glasses are fitted, the bezels surrounding all the instruments being chromed. Black faces with white lettering and pointers are used, and all instruments are illuminated from the rear. The speedometer incorporates both total and trip mileage recorders, the latter reading to 999.9 miles and operated by a knurled knob projecting below the dashboard under the speedometer.

There were several types of speedometer

to take account of different tyre sizes. The number of wheel revolutions per mile is written in small lettering just below the total mileage display; '1180' is probably most common. The speedometer reads to 120mph (or 200kph) and incorporates a small red tell-tale light for headlight main beam. The speedometer was normally situated to the left and the rev counter on the right, but sometimes the positions were reversed. The tachometer, red-lined at 5000rpm and calibrated to 6000rpm, is driven mechanically, by cable from the distributor drive shaft, whereas the speedometer is driven from the side of the gearbox or overdrive unit.

The four subsidiary instruments were situated in the centre panel, the usual layout on home market cars being fuel gauge at top left, oil pressure at top right, ammeter at bottom left and water temperature at bottom right; this layout can vary, particularly on export cars. The fuel gauge is marked in quarters, the oil pressure gauge reads to 100psi and the ammeter (manufactured by Lucas) marked at plus or minus 30 amps. The standard temperature gauge, capillary operated from the thermostat housing, has a middle marking of 185°F to indicate normal running temperature; 90°F is the lowest mark, 230°F the highest. A centigrade calibrated instrument was available.

Post TS 60001 TR3As had this altered interior mirror, with a larger head with protective edging and a longer stalk. The scuttle vent opening knob and its surrounding escutcheon are clearly visible. This car has an amber flasher warning light, but it is possible that this light should in fact be green on this post TS 60001 car. The aeroscreen holding bolts have been deleted on these later TR3As. This car has the earlier TR2 type wiper blades fitted.

Two type WL 11 warning lights are situated between the top two smaller instruments. The left-hand one is red for ignition and 'no charge' warning, and the right-hand one amber for the flashing indicators, although this changed to green on very late TR3As. The central panel incorporates five bakelite knobbed switches, plus an ignition key switch. Three of these switches are in a vertical line in the centre of the panel, with panel lights at the top, the pull-out wiper switch in the middle, and the two-stage pull-and-twist side and headlight switch at the bottom. All had their functions marked in white on black knobs. Late TR3As had a rheostatic panel-light switch. Below this line of switches is the ignition switch, which is key operated and surrounded by a chromed round bezel, as with the other switches. The ignition keys came initially from the 'FA' series, later from the 'FP' series. At the bottom left is the push-in starter button and at bottom right the pull-out choke knob. Overdrive, when fitted, was initially controlled by a pull-out switch (Lucas type PS-7/2) situated to the right of the steering wheel (on RHD cars) and inscribed 'overdrive'. However, concurrently with the fitting of the three-speed overdrive, a drum-shaped 'barrel' flick switch (Lucas type 9RW) was brought in, giving a quicker action. Again, the word

The original type of rear-view mirror, with a rubber pad at its base bearing on the bottom of the windscreen and acting as a screen-steady; the mirror fixing screws are incorrect. The bolts on the scuttle top are for attaching the optional aeroscreens.

'overdrive' was incorporated and the switch was sited in the same place.

The heater has a rotary rheostatic control, the position of which can vary. On those home market cars where a heater was fitted as original equipment, the control is usually found on the right-hand side of the steering wheel, quite near the overdrive switch. In fact the switch hole is always present under the dash trim, even if the heater was not specified. From TS 6157, a scuttle air vent was incorporated, and this was operated by a knob in the centre of the capping rail above the dashboard, the words 'Vent-pull' inscribed on its bezel. Long-door TR2s had an interior bonnet release with the control mounted under the dash-

board on the rear of the front bulkhead, adjacent to the outer side of the driver's footwell.

On TR2s, the grab handle situated above the dashboard and under the top capping on the passenger's side was black plastic covered, but on later cars it became chrome-plated and somewhat fatter in section. The rear-view mirror was bolted to the top of the front bulkhead just behind the windscreen. Its fixings also retained a bracket and rubber pad to act as a central steady point for the windscreen. The mirror had a black finish to its back, stem and screen-steady, and a ball joint adjustment. Cars after TS 60001 had mirrors with longer stalks and slightly larger glasses.

The TR3B and Triumph Italia

These much-misunderstood TR developments deserve a small section to themselves, if only to eradicate some of the surrounding misconceptions.

Despite some contrary beliefs, the TR3B has nothing directly to do with the TR3 'Beta' prototypes. The Betas – between two and five of them depending on who you believe – were produced by the factory as prototypes for the possible future development of the 3A. They featured a 2.2-litre engine, all-synchromesh gearbox, a wider track, bulbous wings to cover the wheels, rack and pinion steering, and a unique front grille and bumper assembly. Production did not materialise, probably because the Sales Department considered that an entirely new body was really needed in addition to mechanical improvements.

The TR3B, on the other hand, was very much a continuation of the TR3A, although the designation TR3B never had official Standard-Triumph sanction. Following the virtual cessation of TR3A production upon the introduction of the TR4 in the autumn of 1961, Triumph's North American distributors came to the conclusion that there would still be a demand for a classically-styled sidescreen two-seater alongside the softer, more luxurious TR4. Such was their influence that Triumph agreed at the beginning of 1962 to produce a further batch of left-hand drive TR3As entirely for this market. The body tooling was removed from Mulliners to the Coventry firm of Forward Radiators, which supplied Triumph with completed bodies for the reintroduced cars.

There were two series of TR3Bs: the first series were numbered from TSF1 to TSF 530L, the second from TCF 1 L to TCF 2804 L. The TSF cars were basically TR3As with virtually no detectable differences, but the TCF cars used the TR4 type all-synchromesh gearbox together with the 2138cc, 86mm bore engine as standard. Both series were badged 'TR3', and were available in a more limited range of colours than those offered for the TR3A (full details of TR3B colours, production figures and dates will be found later in the book).

In fact, not all TR3Bs found their way to North America, for the Triumph Italia was still in limited production in Italy and a further batch of chassis was required for these cars. Thus the last 29 TSF chassis, TSF 502L to TSF 530L, were sent to Vignale and became Italias. These chassis with the

The beautiful Triumph Italia belonging to David Tomlin is seen by the windmill at Brill in Buckinghamshire. Like almost all Italias, this one is left-hand-drive.

The 'M' on the badge stands for Michelotti, but the significance of the crossed flags is not obvious. The source of the light units and bumpers is not known to the author, but no doubt they come from the parts bin of some Italian manufacturer of the period.

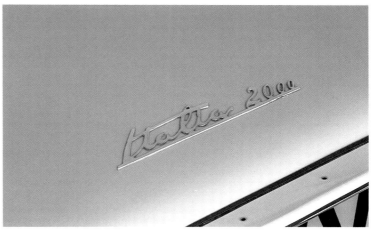

The badges look almost hand-made, which maybe they were. To replace any missing ones would prove a nightmare today!

The Italia's mechanicals are TR3A, with certain modifications. The radiator and thermostat housing are unique to the Italia, and a brake servo is fitted. The trunking feeds a fresh air heater unit.

Carello headlight units and other lamps of Italian manufacture were used on the Italia. The 'Triumph' letters were borrowed from the TR3A, but very few body parts and details were common with other Triumph models.

1991cc engines were particularly sought, as cars under 2-litres were subject to considerably less tax in Italy.

Factory records indicate that there was a considerable overlap between TSF and TCF series production. TCF 1L was built on 8 May 1962, by which date TSF production had only reached TSF 456 L. TSF production then stopped temporarily, but resumed on 7 June 1962, by which time TCF cars had reached TCF 458 L. The last TSF (Italia) chassis was built on 19 September 1962, and the final 'sidescreen' car of all, TCF 2804 L, was probably built in December 1962, more than a year after TR4 production began . . .

Although all TR3Bs were exported, it is now possible to encounter one of these models in the UK, quite a number having been recently reimported.

The Triumph Italia was designed by Michelotti and built in Italy by Vignale Coachworks in Turin. Standard TR3A (and TR3B) chassis were taken from the production line and exported to Vignale, who bodied them with exceptionally pretty fixed-head coupé coachwork, fundamentally of two-seater layout but with a ledge in the rear for small children.

The prototype was shown in 1958, production beginning on a small scale in the summer of 1959. Wire wheels were invariably fitted, and overdrive usually so. It is thought that some, if not all, cars had a special low 4.3:1 rear axle ratio to ensure good performance with the heavier bodywork. The only drawback to this beautiful car was its cost, which at 30–40% more than an equivalently equipped TR3A, inevitably restricted the numbers that could be sold.

Opinions differ over the numbers made. As Vignale's records are not available, it would be necessary to check through tens of thousands of TR build records to establish how many chassis went to Vignale, since they were drawn at random from the production line except for the TR3B batch referred to above. David Tomlin, whose car is illustrated here, feels that the previously quoted figure of 'about 320' is near

The interior shows unmistakeable signs of quality. Upholstery is in leather, the seats being worthy of a luxury saloon. The instruments and the hornpush are from the TR3A, while the wooden steering wheel is probably by Nardi. The flashing indicator lever has slipped round ¼-turn and should be pointing upwards.

An occasional rear bench seat was fitted, the cushion in this car being plain. The front seat backs have zip fasteners, presumably as some form of map pocket or stowage.

The luggage boot was capacious but shallow, the lack of depth caused by spare wheel stowage underneath. Again, the quality of the panelwork and finish is evident.

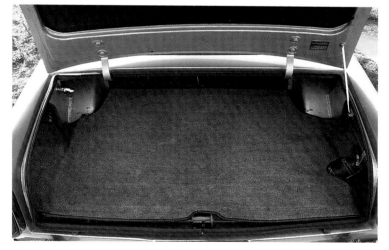

the truth. Certainly, production continued from mid-1959 to late 1962, although new cars were available from unsold stock until well after that time. Of course, by 1962 the Michelotti-designed TR4 could be had with the civilised Surrey hardtop for considerably less money, which did not assist sales of the Italia.

Although quite a number stayed in Italy, many were exported – and quite a few to the USA. Here they took a long time to sell, and prospective buyers were evidently warned by dealers that no stocks of body parts were held in the USA. It is not surprising, therefore, to learn that at least one Italia has surfaced recently with zero miles on the

clock. The model can hardly be considered a success in sales terms, despite its attractive lines.

Despite being principally a left-hand drive car, it seems that a handful of right-hand drive cars – between three and twelve depending upon which source is believed – were built. About half a dozen Italias are known to exist in the UK, but most of these are left-hand drive cars that have been relatively recently imported. The reader will not be amazed to learn that spare body panels, chrome work and other items peculiar to the car are non-existent. Mechnically there are no difficulties, virtually everything being standard TR3A.

Production Changes

Significant changes by commission number (and engine number where appropriate)

TS1
First production TR completed 22/7/53

TS 213 Dec 53
Stronger handbrake assembly fitted.

TS 550 (approx) Feb 54
Aluminium bonnet and spare wheel door deleted, steel items substituted.

TS 869 Mar 54
Improved choke cable assembly fitted.

TS 881E Mar 54
Cross-drilled crankshaft introduced.

TS 995 Mar 54
Windscreen wiper spindle centres increased from 10½in to 14½in.

TS 1201 Apr 54
'Double' thermostat housing deleted and single type substituted, and radiator top hose outlet repositioned. Original range of colours changed, with theoretical deletion of Olive Yellow and Ice Blue. In fact these two colours continued to be available for a further few months.

TS 1307 Apr 54
Original 'squared' type rear light lenses and separate reflectors deleted. New combined rear light lenses and reflectors substituted. Rear wings slightly reprofiled to facilitate fitting of new units.

TS 1391 Apr 54
Additional steering column brace fitted under dashboard.

TS 1869 May 54
Stronger road wheel fitted to avoid previous problem of wheel centres fracturing. Wheels widened to 4½J from 4J. Replacements supplied retrospectively to earlier cars.

TS 1871 May 54
Tonneau cover modified to lengthen zip, allowing cover to be stored more easily behind seats without removal.

TS 1927 Jun 54
Stronger wheel nuts supplied. These were supplied retrospectively to cars manufactured previously.

TS 2532 Jul 54
Longer (24in) silencer box replaces earlier (18in) one.

TS 2673 Jul 54
Rubber cover fitted on overdrive solenoid for waterproofing purposes.

TS 2877 Jul 54
One piece gear lever with separate knob introduced.

TS 3268 Aug 54
Battery box drain tube added.

TS 3512 Sep 54
Radiator protection cross-piece added to front of chassis.

TS 3514 Sep 54
Large 'Tenax' buttons on hood and tonneau replace previous small ones.

TS 4002 Oct 54
'1955' model year cars introduced. Introduction of outer door sills and hence shorter doors better able to clear kerbs when parked. Hardtop became optional, and if specified from new, sliding sidescreens were fitted to allow access to internal door release pulls. Factory 'built-in' provision for hardtop, however, was not made until TS 5260.

TS 4229 Oct 54
Internal cable-operated bonnet release mechanism with two locks, one at each side, deleted on grounds of cost and complication; external Dzus fasteners introduced operated by 'T' shaped carriage key. Bonnet continues to have four air-outlet slots at the rear: although later bonnets had only two outlets, it cannot be established exactly when this change occurred. For a time, bonnets also had a flanged, trailing edge.

TS 4307 Nov 54
Hood now has three-piece rear window, with central window panel now slightly larger.

TS 4310 Nov 54
Chassis reinforced by addition of infill plates and front exhaust mounting modified.

TS 4731 (axle no.)
Crown wheel attachment bolts increased from 5/16in to 3/8in diameter.

TS 4882E Dec 54
Stiffer pistons fitted to engine.

TS 5089 Jan 55
Rubber mats fitted in footwells.

TS 5114 Jan 55
Revised rear hub seals introduced in (only partially successful) attempt to stop oil leakage onto rear brakes.

TS 5255 Feb 55
Sliding sidescreens now supplied to all cars rather than just hardtop-equipped ones. Hinged signalling flap continues, but zip fasteners deleted. Tonneau cover fastenings modified.

TS 5260 Feb 55
Factory now provides built-in provision for fitting of hardtop.

TS 5348 Feb 55
Front hubs strengthened and grease nipples deleted.

TS 5443 Mar 55
Rear brakes increased in diameter from 9in to 10in, handbrake levers on rear brakes modified. Brake shoe width increased from 1¾in to 2¼in.

TS 5469 Mar 55
New design of jack supplied.

TS 5556 Mar 55
Revised rear hubs with bosses increased from 1½in to 1⅝in diameter, necessitating further oil seal change.

TS 5777
Additional steering column brace added, fastening column to one of cross tube bolts.

TS 5980
Uprated overdrive unit fitted, with clutch operating pistons increased in size from 1⅛in to 1⅜in. Still on top gear only. Serial number of new unit 22/1374 and of earlier unit 22/1275.

TS 6157 Apr 55
Introduction of scuttle air vent flap operated from dashboard, together with modified bonnet assembly.

TS 6266 May 55
Three-speed (second/third/top) overdrive unit phased in to replace previous top gear only unit. Barrel-type overdrive flick switch replaces previous pull-out type for quicker operation. Position of switch in dashboard remains similar. All overdrive-equipped cars after TS 6280 have three-speed overdrive.

TS 8039 (axle no)
Uprated nuts fitted to rear hubs to allow for increased tightening torques.

TS 8213 Aug 55
Distributor internals modified including new contact set.

TS 8637 Oct 55
TR3 introduced. Cellular 'eggbox' type radiator aperture grille introduced. Wing beading changed from body coloured, rubberised, fabric type to stainless steel. Chromed hinges for bonnet and boot replaced painted ones. H4 1½in SU carburettors deleted and 1¾in H6 units substituted on inlet manifold modified to suit their four-stud fixings. 'Low port' cylinder head still fitted, but inlet ports slightly opened out, and engine now produced 95bhp instead of 90bhp previously. Front badge changed to suit new designation. Occasional rear bench-type seat now available as optional extra and petrol tank capacity slightly reduced to allow room for this. Inter-carburettor fuel pipe now flexible instead of rigid. Revised range of colours introduced. Sidescreens slightly modified and passenger seat backrest now folds forward to facilitate entry to occasional rear seat. Chrome 'reveal' moulding round 'mouth' now goes right round, rather than finishing at top corners as on late TR2s. The engine number change point for introduction of TR3 was at TS 8997E: rear and centre camshaft bearings were fitted, in addition to front bearing previously specified.

TS 9122 Nov 55
Front lower wishbone bushes changed from rubber to nylon/steel type.

TS 9350 E Nov 55
New cylinder head assembly introduced, based on that developed for TR2s that competed at Le Mans, thus known colloquially as the 'Le Mans' head. Still 'low port' design. Carburettor needles changed to type 'TE'.

TS 9593 Nov 55
Gear lever anti-rattle spring and plunger fitted.

TS 9731E
Even stiffer pistons fitted to engine.

TS 9843 Dec 55
Dynamo: removeable band covering brushgear deleted.

TS 10037E Jan 56
Carburettor needles changed again to type 'SM'.

TS 10132
Front shock absorbers uprated slightly.

TS 11384 May 56
Second silencer introduced instead of previous plain tailpipe.

TS 12567 Jul 56
Windscreen wiper motor, wheelboxes and mounting bracket modified. Now Lucas type DR2 instead of previous CRT 15, fitted on opposite side.

TS 12606 E to TS 13052 Aug 56
Introduction of new 'high-port' cylinder head assembly, manifolds modified to suit. Inlet ports were cast higher up head casting than previously; head casting improved and changed sufficiently to require longer studs to attach it to block. This new assembly helped the engine produce a further 5bhp so that 100bhp could now be quoted. Although the parts book quotes introduction of the 'high-port' head at TS 13052E, in fact it was fitted to some engines on and from TS 12606E at random, so that during this period either type could be fitted to one's new TR3! From TS 13052E it became the standard fitting, and the head design did not alter again during 'sidescreen' TR manufacture.

TS 12650 E Aug 56
Engine oil filter changed from by-pass to full-flow type.

TS 13046 Sep 56
Braking system changed to Girling manufacture, and front disc brakes introduced. Brake and clutch master cylinders changed, as was clutch slave cylinder. Complete rear axle assembly changed from previous Mayflower type to much stronger Vanguard III type, incorporating taper roll-bearings, stronger halfshafts and redesigned hubs to eliminate oil-leakage problems. Rear brakes still 10in × 2¼in, but Girling not Lockheed manufacture, with ¾in rear wheel cylinders (Girling no 390415W). Wire wheel option now fitted with bolt-on hub extensions to replace previous 'hub, peg and collar' system. Commission plate changed from 'square' type to smaller 'oblong' type. Globes on nave plates changed from vitreous enamelled to painted.

TS 15332 Dec 56
Girling rear brakes modified in detail, necessitating new wheel cylinders, still ¾in (Girling no 390416W).

TS 15497 Jan 57
Flexible fuel pipe, petrol tap to fuel pump, modified to simplified design. The petrol tap was later deleted, but it is not certain at what point.

TS 15601 Jan 57
Rear tail light units wired as twin stop lamps (to operate in addition to the central stop lamp) rather than as flashing indicators for USA, Holland and Belgium only. Separate flasher lamps fitted at rear for these markets.

TS 15706 Jan 57
Rear combined tail pipe/silencer further modified to reduce noise.

TS 16473 Feb 57
Rear apron panel part no changes – possibly a new pressing incorporating holes for separate flashing indicators being fitted for USA, Dutch and Belgian markets, and gradually being phased in for other markets. Exact date of their introduction to UK cars remains unclear, but certainly rear panels with pressings for indicators were introduced prior to the TR3A.

TS 18230 E Apr 57
Chromium-plated rocker cover replaces previous painted item, and oil filler/engine breather unit modified.

TS 18913 May 57
Separate number plate lamp replaces combined stop lamp and number plate lamp for USA, Dutch and Belgian markets.

TS 22014 Sep 57
Introduction of 1958 model year cars, unofficially known as TR3As, incorporating numerous detailed changes and improvements. Initial production largely for USA, and cars not available on home market until January 1958. New full-width radiator grille incorporating side/flasher lights, new design front bumper and supports, front apron panel changed so that headlights set further back, air deflector to radiator fitted behind grille (can cause overheating if missing!), exterior lockable door handles and separate orange rear flasher lights standardised. Chrome number plate light fitted, 'Triumph' badging in separate letters fitted front and rear, 'TR3' medallion on front no longer incorporates the word 'Triumph'. New type interior door pulls fitted inside door pockets, new design of seats with thicker backrests and horizontal pleating, revised trim in rear compartment, revised optional occasional rear seat, oblong shape rather than with rounded corners as on the TR3. External lockable boot handle fitted, and budget locks deleted. Petrol tank capacity again slightly reduced to allow more room for rear seat arrangement. Some new colours became available during first few months of production (see separate section). Dashboard centre panel now given black finish rather than matching the rest of dashboard as previously. Wheels now silver/aluminium colour lacquered, rather than body colour. Sidescreen sliding windows lose their external finger grips now that door handles standardized, to make unauthorised entry more difficult. Full tool kit (previously an accessory) becomes standard equipment.

TS 26698E Jan 58
Final development of 'supremely' stiff pistons fitted to engine.

TS 26825 Jan 58
Certain gearbox bearings changed from plain to needle-roller type.

TS 26904 Jan 58
From this point, rear springs (which were previously identical) apparently became 'handed'. The original spring continued for the driver's side, but a new, slightly softer spring was specified for the passenger side, presumably in an attempt to counteract the driver's weight when the car was being driven solo.

TS 28826 Feb 58
Previous 'wedge' type sidescreen fixing sockets deleted, and new Dzus type substituted providing a more positive fixing using the 'T' bar carriage key.

TS 32833 Apr 58
Pre-drilled bolt mountings in scuttle top for fixing aeroscreens deleted.

TS 33894 Jun 58
Rear brake wheel cylinders reduced in size to ⅝in from ¾in to alleviate premature rear wheel locking (Girling no 390400W).

TS 34312 Jun 58
Brake master cylinder seal modified to cure previous excessive pedal travel which had become apparent since seal was previously modified at TS 28000 approx.

TS 41743 Jan 59
Extra fixing eyelet added to tonneau cover.

TS 41878 Jan 59
Front medallion colours changed from red and black to blue and white.

TS 42400 Jan 59
Ashtray fitted as standard.

TS 50001 Apr 59
Gearbox modifications, including new top cover deleting previous gearbox dipstick and substituting an oil level plug. New design of 'short' starter motor fitted where bendix pinion throws opposite way to previously – starter ring gear modified.

TS 56377 Jun 59
Rear brakes reduced in size from 10in × 2¼in to 9in × 1¾in to avoid rear wheel locking problems. Front disc brake calipers changed to Girling 'B' type split units. Rear wheel cylinders increased in size from ⅝in to ¾in bore (Girling no 390415W, again!).

TS 60001 Oct 59
New tooling introduced for bodyshell, probably necessitated by previous body tools wearing out. Many detailed changes incorporated: raised platforms for bonnet and boot hinges, windscreen fixings changed from Dzus type to bolts, rear floor pressings redesigned (petrol tank consequently modified) so that there was a flat platform instead of the previous sloping panels. The occasional rear seat arrangements also had to be modified. Boot floor pressing modified to make more room in spare wheel compartment for larger tyres. Doors incorporated rounded rather than right-angled bottoms to their internal framework. Some windscreen surrounds were now polished cast aluminium rather than chromed.

TS 64561
(possibly body no EB 64561)   Dec 59
Wiring loom changed from fabric to plastic, incorporating 'push-on' type connectors.

TS 71372 E
Clutch slave cylinder and bracket modified.

TS 74331 E
Several changes effected to the thermostat housing.

TS 78718 E
Rocker shaft springs modified.

TR3B Production Changes
TSF2
Minor modifications made to front suspension.

TSF 219
Disc brake caliper mounting plate changed.

TSF 265
Rear shock absorbers modified.

TSF 284
Further minor front suspension modifications.

TCF 1
Dashboard/front bulkhead assembly changed, together with the master cylinder 'pocket'.

Note 1
'L' and 'O' suffixes have been omitted from this list to avoid confusion

Note 2
It is believed that some very late TR3As, as well as all TR3Bs, had different rear brake assemblies, being the TR4 type of 9in diameter and wheel cylinder bore of 0.7in. It has not proved possible to establish how many such cars were so fitted, and from what commission number.

Note 3
Some mystery surrounds the introduction date of the later 'split-type' two piece steering column (not to be confused with the adjustable column available from the start of production – two-piece columns could be both adjustable and non-adjustable!). Study of the Parts Books reveals that the split-type is first mentioned in the 3rd Edition in late 1958, but is not referred to in the supplement consequent upon the TR3A's introduction. Thus the split column must have come in between about TS 26000 and TS 34000, but I cannot be more specific. Nor is it certain whether, once introduced, it became the universal fitment for there is evidence of 'one-piece column' cars being built later in the series. The split-column was introduced to allow easier removal of the steering column. Additional brackets were needed on the chassis to secure the split type column.

Note 4
Some very late TR3As may have had TR4 type front discs, of 10⅝in diameter, which were also fitted to TR3Bs. However it has not so far proved possible to confirm this or identify any change point.

OPTIONS, EXTRAS & ACCESSORIES

A very considerable number of options and extras were available from the factory, together with various 'after-market' accessories produced by independent firms. Quite a few options were available from the start of TR2 production, more being added – especially competition-orientated ones – as the car's suitability for rallying and club racing became apparent.

From the start of TR2 production, or shortly thereafter, the following were available:

Overdrive. Initially on top gear only, but from May 1955 (TS 6266) fitted to second, third and top. The factory made a 'retro-fit' conversion kit available for earlier cars, part nos 501803 (RHD) and 502104 (LHD).

Wire wheels, with centre lock 'knock-off' hubs. Believed only available from January 1954.

Competition front shock absorbers. Part no 113556.

Cast aluminium engine sump. Part no 502126.

Stiffer front springs. Part no 201899.

Larger rear shock absorbers. Part nos 108198 (LH) and 108197 (RH).

Aero-screens. The 'works' type bolted directly to pre-drilled holes in the scuttle – these holes were deleted from TS 32833. Part no 700896.

Undershield. Not a rally-type protective item, but a lightweight aluminium shield under the engine to provide better streamlining – very few were sold, as it promoted overheating and reduced ground clearance! Part no 502122.

Rear wing spats. A 'streamlining' item. Their fitment (only possible with steel disc wheels) caused the rear brakes to overheat in hard use. Part no 552083 for complete kit.

Metal cockpit cover. Again, a 'streamlining' item; a pre-formed aluminium cover to go over the passenger area for high speed work – presumably, they were 'handed'. Very few, if any, were sold, and it does not appear in the August 1954 list.

Interior heater. More early cars built without rather than with, but its fitment became progressively more common. Available also as a 'retro-fit' kit, part no 551877.

Leather upholstery. See 'Interior Trim' section for full details.

Radio. This fitted in the glovebox area, a special 'facia plate assembly' being specified to take the place of the lid. Three radios were available, all by Radiomobile under the HMV name; an Allwave model (part no 552059), Medium Wave only (552058) and Long Wave only (552057). A separate valve unit was employed, usually fitted in the passenger's footwell tunnel, and the loudspeaker was a 6½in 'Hayes' model. From October 1955, a push-button unit could be supplied.

Tool roll and tools. It seems that on TR2s and TR3s only basic wheel-changing items were supplied as standard. The additional tool kit apparently comprised: two tyre levers, grease gun, plug spanner, ½in AF boxspanner, three open ended AF spanners (⅜in × ⁷⁄₁₆in, ½in × ⁹⁄₁₆in and ⅝in × ¾in) tommy bar, pliers, feeler gauge, combination tool (evidently an adjustable spanner!), screwdriver, tyre valve extractor and spare valves. Part no 301413. The Parts Book states that this tool kit became standard equipment on the TR3A.

Telescopic Steering Column. This gave about 3in of in/out adjustment, but most drivers found that it merely brought a wheel that was already close enough even closer! When specified, a different steering wheel was used, with its spokes disposed like the Mercedes-Benz motif, whereas the normal wheel had spokes in a 'T' shape. Part nos 502228 (LHD) and 502231 (RHD).

Road Speed Tyres. Still 5.50 × 15 size, as per standard tyres. Surprisingly, they had a S-T part no of 501532.

Two-Speed Wipers. Part no 501843 up to TS 994, 501956 thereafter. Later cars had a different type of knurled, rotary wiper switch to operate these.

Fitted Suitcase. Specially shaped to make best use of the sloping internal boot area. This item was available in different colours to match the trim! Part no 800608.

Dished Steering Wheel. I can find no further details, and have never seen one.

Full tonneau cover and hoodstick cover. Many different part numbers, to cover all trim colours and LHD or RHD.

Here is the very rare boot-shaped suitcase, sold as an optional extra for the TR2. Brass-bound corners and three white 'Bakelite' handles are fitted. The case came in several colours to match the trim – this one is in faded Geranium. Note also the original boot stay. This is the correct way round to fit it, so that if wind catches the open boot lid, the stay hook catches in the slotted receiving socket. The correct body-coloured wing piping is of the later, larger-section type.

Original steel hardtop, with panoramic rear window. This is Martin King's ex-works car, which explains the rally-type spotlight on the roof. The later sliding sidescreens with fixed lower panels are shown, as are the door handles introduced with the TR3A. The hardtop had chromed rainwater gutters. The car is finished in the Apple Green colour used for works competition and some production TR3As (Bill Piggott photo).

The following additional items were listed as being available in a Standard–Triumph leaflet dated August 1954:

Luggage Grid. This was the early type that bolted to the boot lid. The later type attached to the boot hinges and was clamped at the bottom to the lid, and required no drilling. Part no 552398.

Competition Spark Plugs. Part no 502200. Champion L11S.

Skid plate. This was a 'rally-type' sump-shield, part no 301644.

Hand-operated screen washers. Part no 500898, replaced later by part no 553729, and eventually by vacuum-operated washers.

Windscreen defroster. Electrical element 'stick-on' type, part no 59844.

Wing mirror. Reversible, non-handed type, part no 70326 (later superseded by part no 502459).

Cigarette lighter. Part no 502041.

Licence holder. For use with aeroscreens, part no 602226.

Anti-dazzle interior mirror. Part no 70400.

Tailored link floor mats. Part no 552164. Sold as a set of two, either black or coloured.

Swivelling ashtray. Part no 701019. Fitted under driver's side of dashboard, and swung out for use.

Reversing Light. Part no 502251. Fitted on rear overrider bracket.

Badge Bar. Part no 552399.

Spot Lamp (Lucas). Part no 501703.

Fog Lamp (Lucas). Two types, part nos 501702 and 70377.

Polished wheel rim finisher. Part no 502160. In chrome or polished aluminium, for disc wheels only.

Lower compression kit. Part no 502227. Consisted of a compression plate, shorter pushrods and new gaskets – reduced compression ratio to 7.5 approx. For use in countries with low octane petrol.

By the time the April 1957 list was issued, several more items had become available:

Hardtop kit. Part no 900771, supplied in primer. This was originally introduced in October 1954, made in polyester resin – later the same style of hardtop was manufactured in steel. Both types usually had perspex rear windows, but some glass ones exist.

Seat Covers. The list includes a cryptic note: "priced from £7 10s according to quality".

Continental Touring Kit. Part no 502022.

Radiator Blind. Part no 502866. Cord-operated from dashboard.

Reveal moulding kit. Part no 554331. This is the chrome strip around the 'mouth' of the TR2, available as an extra.

Radiator Grille. Part no 801255. This is the TR3-type cellular grille, available to TR2 owners to 'update' their cars, apparently with official sanction.

Grand Touring conversion kit. Part no 554313. Consisted of external door handles and locks for use in conjunction with the hardtop, principally to make the car eligible for certain competition events. A factory supplement issued relating to this kit is dated 27 March 1956. A chromed strip was also included, to run along the bottom of the sidescreen where it joined the door.

Occasional seat. Part no 801264. This was the TR3 type.

Push-button radio. Medium wave only, part no 552903; Long and Medium Wave, part no 552902.

In addition to the above, the 4.1:1 rear axle ratio (fitted in conjunction with overdrive) became available, both as an original fitting and as a later substitution – but I cannot establish exactly when. Certainly it existed in 'Lockheed' form, and was probably available almost from the start of TR3 production. Similarly, the option of 86mm cylinder liners giving 2138cc became available on TR3As, but again the records are unclear as to when. Both these items were developed by the competition department for rally cars, as were other speed items not specifically referred to in the above lists. Because many competition-minded owners liaised closely with the works and acquired items not, or not initially, available to the public, it is difficult to say which items of competition equipment were factory-offered options or extras.

Alfin aluminium/steel brake drums were available almost from the start of TR production, but they do not appear in the options list other than in a note stating that they should be ordered from Standard-Triumph distributors.

Michelin X radial tyres were available by 1956, and the contemporary fashion for white-wall tyres, especially on USA cars, was also catered for.

The parts book lists an anti-roll bar kit (part no 508397) for the TR3A, but nothing similar is listed for the TR2 or 3.

Some of the items listed in this section undoubtedly did not remain available until the end of production (or beyond), but the records do not usually give dates of deletion.

IDENTIFICATION, DATING & PRODUCTION FIGURES

Very fortunately, Standard-Triumph were extremely logical in the allocation of numbering schemes for their cars and engines. Unlike some manufacturers, Standard-Triumph normally used straight sequences of numbers, starting, amazingly, with 1! Thus it is easy to see where a particular vehicle comes in the production run.

Left- or right-hand drive cars were numbered in the same sequence; LHD cars had an 'L' suffix, whereas RHD cars had nothing. All cars fitted with overdrive from new (whether LHD or RHD) had the suffix letter 'O', this being part of the commission or car number, but separated from the main number on the commission plate by a ½in gap in an attempt to avoid confusion. Unfortunately, confusion still occurs where owners (and licensing authorities) have read this letter 'O' as a zero, a point which needs watching when quoting a commission number.

Standard-Triumph always called the vehicle identification number a commission (or car) number, rather than a chassis number. There is no chassis number as such: many chassis carry a small plate at the front end stamped 'Z28', but this number has no known significance.

The TR2/3/3A production series of numbers normally carried the prefix letters 'TS' (believed to indicate Triumph Sports), the type designation within the factory being '20TR2'. Some cars carry the prefix 'BTS', but this applies to those assembled from Completely Knocked Down kits in Belgium. Such cars are numbered in the standard sequence, but some CKD kit cars assembled in other markets had locally applied number sequences; a 'TS' number was allocated as well, but not always carried on the car. For instance, cars assembled in South Africa have the prefix 'TR', followed usually by a three-figure number – but the 'TS' number does not appear on the vehicle. Chassis exported to Italy for bodying as Triumph Italias carry the suffix letters 'LCO', standing for 'Left-hand drive, Chassis Only'.

TR production began on 22 July 1953 with TS1L'O' (a LHD car with overdrive) and TS2 (a RHD car without overdrive). Numbering then continued, it is thought, without a break up to TS 8636 – the final TR2, built on 6 October 1955. One or two numbers are not found in the factory records, but I believe that this is because the records are incomplete or missing, not because the car was not built.

TR3 numbering continued where the TR2 series ended, the first numbered TR3 being TS 8637, built on 11 October 1955. However, the first TR3 built was TS 8709L on 7 October 1955. Again, the numbering was continuous through to the final TR3, TS 22013, built on 17 September 1957. Type designation on the commission plate changed to '20TR3'.

As is well known, the TR3A was not initially – and never officially – referred to as a TR3A by Standard-Triumph, and was never badged as such. It continued to be called the TR3, and once again the numerical series carried on directly, commencing with TS 22014, also built on 17 September 1957. However, there was a major break during the TR3A numerical sequence, for commission numbers from TS 47956 to TS 50000 inclusive were never issued. Any car purporting to carry a number from this block should be regarded with suspicion. Additionally, for some reason the cars numbered TS 47939 to TS 47955 were built *after* the TS 50001 series numbering was started! Cars then continued to be built in numerical sequence, with occasional lapses where a higher-numbered vehicle was constructed prior to a lower-numbered one, right through to the end of TR3A production at TS 82346 in January 1962. The records indicate the possibility of an additional car, TS 82347, having been built, but this cannot be verified. In 1961, due to a sales slump caused by world recession, very few TR3As were manufactured. Sales that year were supplied largely from the stock of unsold cars built up during the latter part of 1960, some of these cars taking more than a year to sell.

The TR3B cars, made specifically for the USA market and dealt with more fully elsewhere, had numbers in two separate series. The earlier cars were in the series TSF 1 to TSF 530 (although TSF 502 to TSF 530 (although TSF 502 to TSF 530 inclusive were finished as Triumph Italias). The later cars, which had the 2138cc engine as standard, ran from TCF 1 to TCF 2804. All cars had an 'L' suffix as all were left-hand drive. The first TSF car was built on 1 March 1962, but the date of construction of the very last sidescreen TR, TCF 2804, is uncertain as the factory records are missing. However, it is believed that TR3B production finished prior to the end of 1962, probably in December.

TR2/3/3A/3B commission numbers appear on a plate rivetted to the front bulkhead under the bonnet. There are two types of plate; a larger, almost square one (with cut off corners) covers TR2s and early TR3s, while a smaller, oblong one was used on later TR3s and 3As/3Bs.

TR2/3/3A engine numbers also follow a logical numerical sequence. Again, the prefix TS is carried, followed by the number·(commencing at 1) and suffixed by the letter 'E'. As far as can be established, the numerical sequence continued straight through, so there *are* engine numbers in the gap between commission numbers TS 47956 to TS 50000. Whether *all* these blank car numbers have equivalent numbered engines is uncertain.

Since Standard-Triumph supplied engines to outside firms (principally to Morgan for the Plus 4 but also for the Swallow Doretti) and these engines were numbered in the same 'TS . . . E' series, engine numbers were used at a slightly faster rate than car numbers. Thus the engine original to a particular car will always have a 'TS . . . E' number higher than the TS number of the car itself. This gap grows progressively during production, to the point where later cars will have an engine number several hundreds higher than the commission number.

The factory operated an exchange engine rebuild scheme, such engines having an 'FR' suffix to indicate 'Factory Rebuilt'. In these cases, the details of crank journal and piston size were given on a stamped plate fixed to the engine over the top of the original number. Original 'TS . . . E' engine numbers themselves were stamped on the block, just below cylinder head level on the

The commission plate as fitted to TR2s and early TR3s – basically square but with the corners 'nibbled'. The four holding rivets are correct.

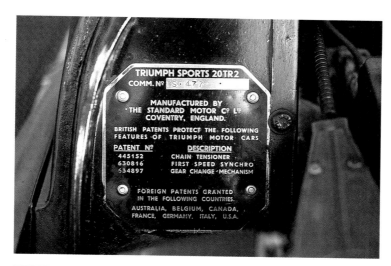

The later TR3/3A commission plate is much smaller and has only two rivets instead of four. The weight is given only in kilos, as early as 1957! It is believed that this was because the weight had to be stated only for the German market. The black fluid reservoir would originally have had a transfer on it indicating 'brake' and 'clutch'.

right-hand side of the engine as viewed from the front. These stampings can be very difficult to decipher on some blocks. TR3B engines also had the 'E' suffix, but were prefixed 'TSF' or 'TCF' as appropriate. Some TRs, unfortunately, have been fitted with Standard Vanguard engines over the years, so any engine not carrying the correct 'TS' prefix and 'E' suffix – unless a factory rebuilt or TR3B engine – should be regarded as suspect.

TR2/3/3A bodies carry two numbers, both on small brass plates rivetted or screwed to the front bulkhead just above the battery tray. One of these plates has an 'EB' prefix and a number near, but slightly higher than, the car's commission number. The other plate has a straight six- or seven-figure number with neither prefix nor suffix. Only this latter number appears in the factory build records held by the British Motor Industry Heritage Trust, and little is known about the allocation or series of either body number.

I have been told that the six- or seven-figure number was allocated to the bare bodyshell by Mulliners, the manufacturers, whereas the 'EB' number is a Standard-Triumph one allocated to the complete trimmed body. Certainly this theory seems to be borne out by the fact that the 'EB' number roughly accords with the car's commission number, whereas the other number appears to have no connection. The fact that the 'EB' number is higher than the commission number could be explained by numbers being allocated to spare bodies used for repairing damaged vehicles. However, little can be learned at present from either body number, although possibly in the future some more information may materialise.

One final and intriguing point relating to TR numbers remains to be revealed. My research has turned up three (so far) TR2s listed in the records as 'Speed Models', which apparently had the additional suffix letters 'SP' after their commission numbers. I have never seen any other mention of such cars and their specification is a matter of

conjecture, but I suspect they may have been replicas of the 124mph 'Jabbeke' car, MVC575, possibly with undershields and metal tonneau covers. Whether the 'SP' suffix was actually stamped on the commission plate I cannot say, not having encountered one, but it seems that these mysterious cars were made. One, an Earls Court Motor Show car in October 1953, is listed in the records as TS19L (SP) O, indicating a left-hand drive speed model fitted with overdrive.

Dating a TR should present no problem, although this can only be done accurately from the commission number, or reasonably approximately from the engine number if the car carries its original engine. Factory records allow exact dating from the commission number, but the table below gives a rough idea.

1953	Production started at TS1 LO on 22/7/53
1954	First car in year, TS 306 L, built 1/1/54
1955	First car in year, TS 5203 LO, built 4/1/55
	Last TR2, TS 8636, built 6/10/55
	First TR3, TS 8637, built 11/10/55
1956	First car in year, TS 9666-O, built 2/1/56
1957	First car in year, TS 14999 L, built 1/1/57
	Last TR3, TS 22013, built 17/9/57
	First TR3A TS 22014, built 17/9/57
1958	First car in year, TS 25633 L, built 1/1/58
1959	First car in year, TS 41668 L, built 1/1/58
1960	First car in year, TS 65124★
1961	First car in year, TS 82030★
1962	First car in year, TS 82340
	Last car TS 82346 (possibly TS 82347, see above)

★ The factory records at these points are not complete, so these numbers have been taken from an alternative source. Towards the end of TR3A production, chassis numbers were also often built out of sequence, so numbers built in a year do not exactly tally with numbers allocated. An engine can be roughly dated using the above table, bearing in mind that engine numbers were always slightly ahead of commission numbers.

As for production figures, the accompanying table is as accurate as I can obtain from the available records, taking into account the 2044 'missing' numbers between TS 47956 and TS 50000 inclusive.

Unfortunately, an accurate split between left- and right-hand drive cars cannot be established, at least not without individually examining every car's build record, which, with more than 80,000 built, no-one has yet had time to attempt! Statistics, however, do exist for years from 1953 to 1961 showing the mix of home and export deliveries. One must also bear in mind that quite a number of right-hand drive cars were exported.

Taking 1953 and 1954 together, the factory records indicate that 2973 TR2s were exported from a total manufactured of 5202 – roughly 57 per cent. Delivery destinations were extremely varied, the greatest number (1451 cars) going to the USA, with the remaining cars spread over more than 70 countries! Canada, Belgium, France, Germany and Australia were the next biggest markets in descending order, with several countries – such as Ecuador, Haiti, Mauritius, New Guinea and French West Africa – taking single examples. Some of the cars sent to Belgium were partially rebodied as fixed-head coupés, called TR2 Francorchamps; it is believed 22 such cars were built.

I suspect that cars delivered in the UK to US service personnel and other foreign nationals based here are not included in the above export total to the USA, even though such cars were in fact exported by their owners. This would explain a discrepancy that I have found – namely that significantly more early TR2s appear to have been built left-hand drive than were recorded as exported in the factory records! As TR production increased and progressed through the 1950s, the proportion of cars exported grew considerably, until by 1959/60 the home market accounted for only 3–5 per cent of deliveries. Of the 21,186 cars made in 1959, 20,440 were exported complete, 108 were exported as CKD kits and a mere 638 stayed in the UK. The best year for TR2/3/3A production was 1959, although 1958 and 1960 were nearly as good. Although the full breakdown of car delivery destinations is not available, I estimate that by 1959 more than 85 per cent of all TRs were going to North America. In fact, fewer TR3As than TR2s were sold in the UK, despite the 3A being in production for twice as long and roughly seven times as many being made. Truly an export success!

COLOUR SCHEMES

TR2/3/3A/3B colour combinations for body and trim are complex, but as this is the subject most frequently raised by restorers I shall devote considerable space to them. Fortunately, the surviving factory records are reasonably complete, although there is an occasional gap where supposition has to be made. Detailed research has revealed some previously unknown facts, such as cars painted Sunset Red or the mysterious colour of Jay Blue.

Neither metallic colours nor two-tone colour schemes were offered by the factory, although such cars do exist. To this must be added the caveat that one could order special finishes at extra cost, but the records reveal that this was very rarely done. In addition, quite a number of cars were supplied as Completely Knocked Down (CKD) kits for assembly abroad, and these bodies would probably have been dispatched in primer. The factory, therefore, had no control over (nor records of) what finishing colours were used upon assembly.

Steel disc wheels on TR2s and TR3s were painted the same colour as the bodywork, a practice which visually suited the car. However, from the introduction of the TR3A, silver-coloured lacquer or aluminium-coloured paint was employed, similar to that used for finishing the optional extra wire wheels.

Early TR2s were finished in some bizarre colours, particularly the Geranium Pink and Olive Yellow. There was also an Ice Blue that was not blue at all – rather a light greyish-green. It has been suggested that these colours were chosen by Lady Black, wife of the Standard-Triumph Chairman, at a time when this car was envisaged more as a 'boulevard cruiser' than as the true sports car it quickly proved itself to be. These colours were quickly dropped and more suitable colours such as British Racing Green and Signal Red substituted.

Two ranges of colours were issued during TR2 production. The car was launched with the colours referred to in a factory list dated 23 July 1953 (see Table 1). This list was superseded at BEC 115 (Body Engineering Change) in April 1954, at TS 1200. On 5 April 1954, a second list of paint and trim colours, current from TS 1201 to the end of TR2 production at TS 8636, was issued (see Table 2). Some qualifying comments are made in the footnotes to these tables.

A third colour list was dated 20 October 1955 (BEC 192) and coincided with the introduction of the TR3 at TS 8637 (see Table 3).

The first TR3A, TS 22014, was built on 17 September 1957, but no trace of a new colour list applicable to this model can be found. Some TR3 colours not generally thought of as available for the TR3A were in fact continued onto the new cars, and some new TR3A colours – for example, Primrose Yellow and Powder Blue – were not immediately available. From my study of the factory build records, I have been able to construct the list in Table 4. Additionally, it should be noted that no specific body/hardtop colour combinations were laid down for the TR3A, a note in the records stating that 'any approved colour as scheduled by the sales department' was available for hardtops.

PRODUCTION FIGURES

	TR2	TR3	TR3A	TR3B	Total
1953	305				305
1954	4897				4897
1955	3434	1029			4463
1956		5333			5333
1957		7015	3619		10634
1958			16035		16035
1959			21186		21186
1960			17054		17054
1961			408		408
1962			7	3334	3341
Total	8636	13377	58309 (incl. Italias)	3334 (incl. Italias)	83656

Note: the above totals include CKD cars supplied for local assembly, and also TR3A/Bs supplied in chassis only form for Triumph Italias.

As will be apparent from Table 4, there was something of an 'anything goes' philosophy with TR3A paint/trim colours during the 1957/58 model year. However, the position was regularised in September 1958 (approximately at TS 37000) when the new colour list described in Table 5 was issued, although not all colours were available straight away. It should be noted that any of the hardtop, hood/sidescreen and trim colours quoted in Table 5 for each particular body colour be supplied in any combination for that body colour. For example, a Black car could be ordered with a Powder Blue hardtop, Targo Purple trim and Beige sidescreens! Clearly this could have led to

some unpleasant combinations being ordered, but one presumes that the factory had some faith in the good taste of its customers!

A limited range of four paint colours was available for the TR3B (see Table 6). These were similar to the early TR4 colours, except that no British Racing Green cars have been found in the records. So few hardtop-equipped cars have been found in the records that a worthwhile list cannot be supplied.

Paints were principally supplied by the firm of Dockers Ltd, later taken over by Pinchin-Johnson Ltd (a division of Courtaulds Ltd), who might be able to help with

requests from restorers. If possible, a chip of the original colour should be supplied for matching purposes (original unfaded paint can sometimes be found under the bulkhead area).

Details of paint reference numbers are given in Table 7. Although the reference numbers will no longer be current, clearly it is worth quoting as much information as possible. Where more than one reference is given for the same colour for the same manufacturer, there may be more than one shade – considerable care will be needed to ensure an exact match. Alternatively, the other numbers quoted can refer to a different type of paint in the same shade.

TABLE 1
TR2 colours up to TS 1200 (list dated 23/7/53)

Paint	Trim	Hood and sidescreens
Ice Blue	Grey	Ice Blue
	Blackberry	Blackberry
	Geranium	Geranium
Geranium	Grey	Ice Blue
	Blackberry	Blackberry
	Geranium	Geranium
Olive Yellow	Grey	Ice Blue
	Blackberry	Blackberry
	Geranium	Geranium
Pearl White	Geranium	Geranium
	Grey	White
	Blackberry	Blackberry
Black	Geranium	Ice Blue, Blackberry, Pearl White
	Grey	Ice Blue, Blackberry, Pearl White
	Blackberry	Ice Blue, Blackberry, Pearl White

Notes
1. The factory specifications state that leather or Vynide trim was available throughout the currency of the above range. In fact, the first 150 cars were built with leather trim, TS 151 being the first Vynide car.
2. There were also some 'trial colour' cars built: TS 369 was painted Signal Red and TS 413 British Racing Green. Both later became standard colours.

TABLE 2
TR2 colours from TS 1201 to TS 8636 (list dated 5/4/54)

Paint	Trim	Hood and sidescreens
Signal Red	Brown	Fawn, Black
	Stone[2]	Fawn
	Red	Fawn (and possibly Black)
British Racing Green	Red	Fawn, Black
	Brown	Fawn, Black
	Stone[2]	Fawn
Black	Brown	Fawn, Black
	Blue	Fawn, Black
	Red	Fawn, Black
	Stone[2]	Fawn
	Grey	Fawn (and possibly Black)
Pearl White	Blue	Fawn, Black
	Red	Fawn, Black
	Brown	Fawn, Black
	Grey	Fawn, Black
Geranium	Geranium	Geranium, Black, Fawn
	Grey	Geranium, Black, Fawn

Notes
1. Although the factory hardtop was available from October 1954, there is no reference to its colour availability until the TR3's introduction in October 1955 (see Table 3).
2. Stone trim was available in leather only. A note in the records states 'to use up existing stocks', so presumably it was not available through the entire period of this colour range. Otherwise, all trim colours were available in hide or Vynide.
3. Factory records make it clear that the above list is not exhaustive, in that Olive Yellow and Ice Blue cars *were* built after their supposed deletion, possibly to special order. For instance, TS 1911 (LO) was built in Olive Yellow and TS 1912 (LO) was built in Ice Blue, both on 26 May 1954. Ice Blue continued for some time thereafter.
4. Geranium was deleted from this list some time during its currency, but the records do not state when. I have never heard of a short door car (after TS 4002) built in this colour, so I suspect it was deleted in late summer 1954.
5. Some older trim colours (Blackberry and Geranium) apparently continued to be used with the April 1954 list through the summer of 1954, presumably to use up otherwise redundant trim stocks.

TABLE 3
TR3 colours (list dated 20/10/55)

Paint	Trim	Hood and sidescreens[1]
Black	Blue, Beige, Red, Black Brown, Vermillion, Stone, Grey	Fawn, Black
Signal Red	Beige, Red, Black, Brown, Vermillion, Stone, Grey	Fawn, Black
BRG	Beige, Red, Black, Brown, Vermillion, Stone, Grey	Fawn, Black
Pearl White	Blue, Red, Black, Brown Vermillion	Fawn, Black
Salvador Blue[3]	Blue, Red, Black, Vermillion Stone, Grey	Fawn, Black
Beige[5]	Blue, Beige, Red, Black, Brown, Vermillion, Stone	Fawn, Black
Apple Green[4]	Beige, Red, Black, Brown, Vermillion, Stone	Fawn, Black

TR3 hardtop colour combinations[2]

Paint	Hardtop	Trim	Sidescreens
Black	Black	Blue, Red, Brown, Stone	Black
Pearl White	Pearl White	Blue Red, Brown	White
	Black	Blue, Red, Brown	Black
BRG	BRG	Red, Brown, Stone	Fawn, Black
	Black	Red, Brown, Stone	Black
Signal Red	Signal Red	Brown, Stone	Fawn, Black
	Black	Brown, Stone	Black
Salvador Blue[3]	Salvador Blue[3]	Blue, Red, Stone	Fawn
	Black	Blue, Red, Stone	Black
Beige	Beige	Brown, Vermillion, Stone	Fawn
	Sunset Red[6]	Brown, Vermillion, Stone	Fawn
Apple Green[4]	Apple Green[4]	Stone	Fawn

Notes
1. Hood and sidescreens were also available in White to special order only.
2. The factory records contain this note: 'The hardtop shade with Black-trimmed cars is not stated, and it should be flexible for customers to have a choice from the complete range of shades approved for hardtop models'.
3. Salvador Blue was superseded in September 1956 by Winchester Blue. Beige and Brown were added to the existing choice of trim colours for cars supplied without hardtops.
4. Although the colour is not mentioned in the original records as being available, I have added Apple Green both for body and hardtop colours as the build records definitely prove it was supplied, not only for works competition cars but also for ordinary customers. The exact date of introduction is unclear, but I would guess autumn 1956.
5. The build records prove that some non-hardtop cars were supplied in Beige, although it used to be thought that cars came in this colour only when supplied with hardtops as original fitments.
6. Sunset Red appears as a new hardtop colour. No mention is made in the factory list of its being available as a body colour. However, the records reveal that some TR3s (and early 3As) *were* supplied painted Sunset Red – for instance TS 20965 (O) built on 16 August 1957.
7. The factory build records reveal that at least two TR3s were painted in a colour called Jay Blue – TS 20322 (L) and TS 21218, for instance. I can find no reference elsewhere to such a colour. Also, TS 20424 is described as Ivory – again, I have found no further reference to this colour.

TABLE 4
TR3A (colours from TS 22014, Sept 1957 to Sept 1958)

Paint	Trim[1]	Hood and sidescreens[2]
Pearl White	—	—
BRG	—	—
Pearl Grey	—	—
Winchester Blue[3]	—	—
Signal Red	—	—
Sunset Red[4]	—	—
Powder Blue[5]	—	—
Black	—	—
Apple Green[6]	—	—
Beige[3]	—	—
Primrose Yellow[7]	—	—

Notes
1. A note in the records states: 'Any approved trim colour may be fitted to any body paint colour combination as scheduled by the sales department'. The approved colours appear to have been Red, Blue, Black, Beige and Grey – and later Targo Purple and Silverstone Grey.
2. A note in the records concerning hood and sidescreen colours states: 'Any approved colour is acceptable – Black, Beige or White as scheduled by the sales department'.
3. Beige and Winchester Blue appeared on quite a number of US-bound TR3As during the early months of production, but very few, if any, RHD cars appear to have been built in these colours. Both colours were discontinued in November 1957.
4. Sunset Red, previously thought to have been a hardtop colour only, appears as the body colour of quite a few TR3As built in October 1957, and seems to have been offered alongside rather than in place of Signal Red. Discontinued November 1957.
5. A trial car in Powder Blue (TS 22121) was built on 20/9/57, but the first production Powder Blue car does not appear until TS 24707(L), built 2/12/57.
6. Apple Green TR3As were made in significant numbers – it is not certain whether the colour continued right through to September 1958.
7. A trial car in Primrose Yellow was built on 17/9/57 as TS 22045(O), but the first production car in Primrose Yellow was not built until 24/1/58 as TS 26657(L).

TABLE 6
TR3B colours

Paint	Trim	Hood and sidescreens
Spa White	Black, Red, Midnight Blue	Black, White
Powder Blue	Midnight Blue, Black	Black, White
Black	Red, Black	Black, White
Signal Red	Black, Red	Black, White

Notes
1. TSF cars normally had leather trim, but most TCF cars were trimmed in Vynide.

TABLE 5
TR3A colours (from Sept 1958, approx TS 37000)

Paint	Trim	Hardtop	Hood and sidescreens
Black	Red, Blue, Black, Silverstone Grey[2], Targo Purple[2]	Black, Signal Red, Powder Blue, Pale Yellow, Sebring White[4], Silverstone Grey[3]	White, Black, Beige
Signal Red	Red, Black, Silverstone Grey[2]	Black, Signal Red, Sebring White[4]	White, Black
BRG	Red, Silverstone Grey[2], Targo Purple[2]	Black, BRG, Sebring White[4], Silverstone Grey[3]	White, Black, Beige
Pale Yellow[1]	Black, Silverstone Grey[2], Targo Purple[2], Red	Black, Pale Yellow, Sebring White[4]	White, Black
Powder Blue	Blue, Black	Black, Powder Blue, Sebring White[4]	White, Black
Sebring White[1,4]	Red, Blue, Black, Silverstone Grey[2] Targo Purple[2]	Black, Signal Red, BRG, Sebring White[4]	White, Black
Silverstone Grey[1]	Silverstone Grey[2], Targo Purple[2], Red	White, BRG, Sebring White[4], Silverstone Grey[3]	Black

Notes

1. New colours appeared in approximately January 1959: Pale Yellow replaced Primrose Yellow; Sebring White replaced Pearl White; Silverstone Grey replaced Pearl Grey.
2. No other significant changes to this list were made until June 1960 (at TS 77000 approximately), when Targo Purple and Silverstone Grey were deleted as trim colours. The possibility of Pale Yellow bodywork with Red trim was also deleted at this time – thankfully!
3. The records also show that Silverstone Grey was deleted as a hardtop colour in June 1960, but nothing is said regarding this colour as a car body colour. It must be assumed that it remained available until the end of TR3A production.
4. The only addition to the list in June 1960 was Spa White. It is clear from the records that this colour replaced Sebring White for hardtops (24/6/60), but apparently Sebring White continued for car bodies for some time – such that for a period a Sebring White car could be ordered with a Spa White hardtop! Spa White eventually replaced Sebring White for car bodies, but I cannot establish when; trim colours remained the same.

TABLE 7
TR2/3/3A/3B paint codes

Paint	Reference numbers
Ice Blue	Dockers BF 4575
Geranium	Dockers BF 4863
Olive Yellow	Dockers BF 4862
Pearl White	Dockers BF 4861, BF 5460, BF 4881, CGW18 or CHW4; ICI HILUX M-048-2857; Pinchin-Johnson PJ 414HS or PJ 414LB; GIP Ltd GLS 5525; Berger (Ault and Wiborg) possibly 17414.
Black	Dockers BF 4695, BF 5516, BF 5956, CGX16 or CHX3; ICI HILUX M-048-122; Pinchin-Johnson PJ 412HS or PJ 412LB.
Signal Red	Dockers BF 5093, BF 5468, BF 5368, CGR33 or CHR 14; ICI HILUX M-048-2859; Pinchin-Johnson PJ 427HS or PJ 427LB; Berger (Ault and Wiborg) 1/18338.
BRG	Dockers BF 5092, BF 5761, BF 5531, CGG40 or CHG65; ICI HILUX M-048-2855; Pinchin-Johnson PJ 428HS or PJ 428LB.
Salvador Blue	Dockers BF 5323; ICI-2759.
Winchester Blue	Dockers BF 5944; ICI-2922.
Pearl Grey	Dockers CHN121; ICI HILUX 2931; Berger (Ault and Wiborg) 40.1346.
Beige	Dockers BF 5967 or BF 5992.
Apple Green	GIP Ltd GLS 5454; ICI 2920 or 2472; Berger (Ault and Wiborg) 18353.
Sunset Red	Dockers BF 5968, BF 6465 or BF 6477.
Powder Blue	Dockers CGB77 or CHC 38; ICI HILUX M-048-8013; Pinchin-Johnson PJ 426HS or PJ 426LB; Berger (Ault and Wiborg) 20539.
Primrose Yellow	Dockers CGC45 or CHX38; ICI HILUX M-048-3220; Pinchin-Johnson PJ 425HS or PJ 425LB; Berger (Ault and Wiborg), possibly 20589; GIP Ltd GLS 5592.
Pale Yellow	Not found in records
Sebring White	Standard-Triumph paint no 555069; ICI 3276; Berger (Ault and Wiborg), 20884.
Silverstone Grey	Standard-Triumph paint no 555072; ICI 3277.
Spa White	Standard-Triumph paint no 555017 or 565020, ICI 3436.
Aluminium/Silver Wheel Paint	Ref. CD31568 (believed Dockers).

Triumph TR4/4A/5/250/6

CHASSIS

Two distinct chassis types were fitted under these cars. The TR4 had a developed version of the 'sidescreen' car chassis, whereas later cars with independent rear suspension required a chassis that differed considerably. Within this latter group was also found a 'crossbreed' version which allowed live axle rear suspension to be fitted to some North American specification TR4As.

The previous description of the TR2/3/3A chassis holds good for the TR4, with the following differences: the front track was increased by 4in, to 49in, and the rear track by 3in, to 48in. At the rear, this merely involved utilising an axle with longer tubes and halfshafts. At the front, the extra 4in was gained by extending the front box-section chassis rails outwards by 2in on each side with welded-on channel sections – extra stiffness was an incidental bonus. The wheelbase remained the same as the TR3A at 88in.

The front suspension towers were re-positioned slightly, and two members were welded to the top of the front chassis rails, angled inwards at their tops and positioned at their bases just forward of the main front cross-member. These carried the rack for the new rack and pinion steering system. The old brackets for the previous type of steering were deleted, together with the front small-diameter cross-tube. Forward body mounts were welded to the extreme front of the chassis rails. The body mounting tubular outriggers required extension

pieces to cope with the wider body, but the main chassis rails remained the same distance apart as on the earlier cars. It is even possible – and has been done! – to fit a TR3A body onto a TR4 chassis with surprisingly little adaptation. The front suspension members and steering geometry were carried over to the TR4, although further reinforcement was added to the rear shock absorber mounting points.

The chassis frame developed for the TR4A, and used with detail differences up to the TR6, was quite different since independent rear suspension necessitated a total re-design. Viewed from above, the new IRS chassis – illustrated in the accompanying diagram from the TR4A parts catalogue – has been rightly described as resembling a bell in front of an 'A' shaped extension, the rear legs of which form the rear chassis rails.

Box section members were again used, but ran parallel only at the extreme front. The chassis frame was very narrow at the point where the 'bell' shape met the 'A' shape, compromising torsional stiffness. Just after the point where the chassis began to widen out to the rear, a large bridge piece standing on two towers was welded across to form the top retaining member for the rear coil springs. At the point where the rear main members become almost parallel, a second 'bridge' type cross-member was fixed, this one serving as a carrier for the rear dampers and a location for the differential casing by means of two rubber-mounted rearward-facing lugs. Two further lugs located the front of the differen-

The pristine TR4 of Derek Pollock.

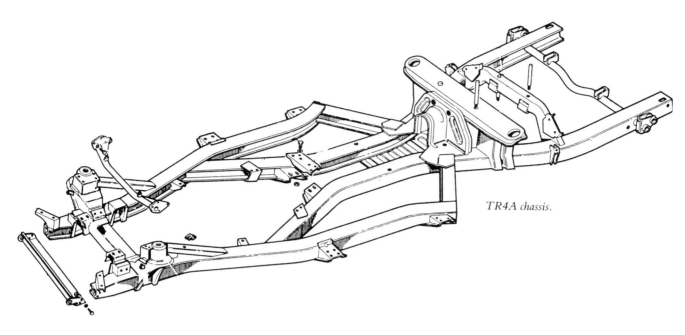

TR4A chassis.

tial casing on the spring-retaining suspension bridge. A final tubular cross-member, passing through the chassis side rails, was located roughly 12in from the rear of the chassis frame; this carried exhaust hanging points together with body mounts at the outer ends of the tube.

Through the centre of the 'bell' passed the rear frame side members, such that for about 3ft of its length the chassis had four box-section members side by side viewed from above, rather than the more usual two. The joining point under the rear of the floors was plated in for strength, a hoop to accommodate the propellor shaft being added on the TR4As. Body mounting brackets were attached to the outer side members, and a bolted in gearbox cross-member connected the two inner side members at a point a few inches aft of their join with the outer side members. Just forward of this point, the forward-facing bracing members that connected to the tops of the front suspension towers themselves met the chassis side rails. The front suspension towers were similar in principle and function to those of the earlier cars, but different in detail; at their base was the main box-section front cross-member. Just in front of this steering rack mounts were welded to the chassis rails, and a bolted-in cross-tube connected the tops of the suspension towers as previously. A radiator protection shield remained and was bolted in place at the extreme front of the chassis frame. There was no longer any need for TR4-style side extension channel sections at the front of the

chassis, as the opportunity had been taken during the redesign to widen the distance between the front chassis rails. Body mounting brackets were fitted at the extreme front of the chassis.

This basic design of IRS chassis was also employed for the TR5/250 and TR6, with only minor differences necessitated principally by the longer six-cylinder engine. The bolted-in cross-tube was bowed somewhat to accommodate the increased engine length, while the steering rack position was also moved and the 'hoop' over the differential area was deleted. In use, however, this chassis proved not to be as torsionally stiff as the TR4 chassis, a fact frequently commented upon by contemporary road testers. When one views the two types of chassis together, it is not difficult to see why, with its thin 'waist' about two-thirds of the way back, the later chassis is less rigid.

I have already mentioned the curious North American specification TR4A with a solid rear axle. This derivative, like the TR3B, was rather forced on Triumph by its US distributors, who felt that IRS represented an uneccessary complication that their customers would neither appreciate nor pay for! Thus the option of a conventionally-sprung TR4A arose just for this market – both types were sold side by side.

The chassis for the live axle car was a modified TR4A type. Provision for semielliptic springs was made by new brackets, carrying the forward ends of the springs, attached to the chassis rails forming the bot-

tom of the 'bell' shape. The rear of the springs attached to conventional swinging shackles mounted on the tubular rear cross-member, very much in the style of the 'sidescreen' cars. Dampers were still mounted on their bridge-piece, but the larger bridge-piece for the coil springs on IRS cars was deleted, the solid axle crossing above the chassis at this point.

FRONT SUSPENSION

The first TR4s used the same front suspension as the last TR3As and Bs, even down to geometry and spring rates; virtually all parts are interchangeable. Even the substitution of rack and pinion steering did not directly affect the suspension design. However, from commission numbers CT 4388 (disc wheels) and CT 4390 (wire wheels) new steering geometry was substituted and the top wishbones had new-style pressings. Front dampers on both types remained telescopic, set within the springs.

A detailed description of the front suspension is found in the TR2/3/3A section. The design of the front suspension remained fundamentally unaltered right through to the TR6, with only detailed differences.

On TR4s from CT 6344 (disc wheels) and CT 6389 (wire wheels), different upper wishbones and ball joints were again fitted, the steering tie rod levers and bottom trunnions also being modified. A 3° castor angle was adopted to aid steering self-centring at speed. Trunnion to lower wishbone grease seals were modified at CT 7218. The front coil springs were lengthened at CT 29984, allowing the large packing pieces that had been sited above the springs to be deleted. Ignorance about the two types of front spring and the use of packing pieces has led to puzzlement among home mechanics, who have wondered at the eccentric front ride heights of their TR4s! Several specifications of front shock absorber were fitted to the TR4, including a type designed for the USA only.

Upon the introduction of the TR4A, a significant – and unfortunate in retrospect – modification was made to the front lower wishbone inner fulcrum points. Whereas the TR4 had used the proven TR3 type with pivot pins forming part of the chassis, for the 4A and later cars, which were deemed to require an altered roll-centre, a simple bracket, bolt and bush arrangement was employed as the lower inner wishbone fulcrum point, both for the front and rear attachments. These brackets were bolted to the front chassis rails, initially with one bolt but later with two. While the system had the required effect on the roll-centre, it proved in later years to be vulnerable to the bolts pulling straight out of a chassis weakened by rust and fatigue – or even to the chassis itself fracturing – with alarming and potentially lethal consequences. The use of wider wheels and tyres over the years has accentuated this tendency, but strengthened parts are now available. Any TR4A/5/6 owner should examine this area of his car regularly.

As with the TR4, the TR4A used differing types of front coil springs, some with packing pieces. Careful study of the parts catalogue is necessary to obtain correct ride height. TR5s had mildly uprated coil springs to handle the increased weight and power of the six-cylinder engine, but in other respects the TR4A front suspension was unaltered.

For the TR6, however, the anti-roll bar, which had been an option for many years, at last became standard. It was attached to the lower wishbones by a drop link and to the front of the chassis frame by 'U' bolts and brackets. Yet again, differing front springs were employed for the TR6. In particular, the US carburettor car's front springs differed from those of the injected cars.

REAR SUSPENSION

Two very different types of rear springing are found on these cars. The TR4 has a system that is, except for small detailed differences, the same as that fitted to the 'sidescreen' cars and described in the previous chapter. Even the rates of the semi-elliptic springs initially remained the same as the earlier car, although the springing effectively became softer because the TR4 was roughly 70lb heavier at the rear. Rear springs, however, were changed early in the TR4's run, at CT 2829; at this point, two identical rear springs were fitted, whereas previously they had had differing rates. Rear springs were changed again at CT 23383, the 'deep-dished' type of spring being introduced with aluminium packing between the spring and axle. The rear axle check strap was modified, and the spring 'eye-to-eye' distance was reduced, necessitating a minor chassis change. Rear shock absorbers were modified at CT 3434 and again at CT 11479; the last type was common with those then being used on the TR3B. After the change at CT 3434, a different specification of rear shock absorber was utilised for US-bound cars.

The arrival of the TR4A in early 1965 introduced independent rear suspension in conjunction with the redesigned chassis frame described earlier, the principles of the IRS being borrowed from the Triumph 2000 saloon that had been introduced 18 months previously. This suspension continued to the end of TR6 production, with limited modification.

The rear wheels are carried on large cast-alloy semi-trailing wishbones, each pivoted on bolts and bushes running in backwards-facing brackets (two on each side) fixed to the chassis frame. A single coil spring on each side bears on the wishbone's upper face at its lower end, and is restrained at its top end by a large transverse chassis bridge piece. A conical rubber bump stop was fitted to the underside of the body on each side, bearing on the wishbone itself in full-bump conditions. Lever-arm shock absorbers were mounted laterally, and at a 45° angle, on a second bridge piece which also formed a chassis cross-member. The arms of the dampers were connected to the trailing edge of the wishbone by rubber bushed drop-links. Two types of rear spring were fitted to the TR4A: a short spring with a spacer piece, and subsequently a long spring without.

The 'trailing wishbone' design was a great advance on the Herald type of swing-axle IRS, and had the virtue of avoiding the violent camber changes to which cheaper forms of IRS are prone. The rear suspension, however, did turn out to be rather soft compared with earlier TRs – tail-squat under acceleration was a particular feature of all independently sprung TRs. Under static unladen conditions, a slight positive camber of around 1° was built into the suspension, but this could be seen to increase under heavy loads or cornering forces. Vertical wheel movement, of course, was considerably increased over the TR3A/4 design, with a consequent increase in comfort and roadholding, albeit at the price of increased complexity and expense. Ground clearance remained the same as the TR4 at 6in.

On the TR5, stiffer rear springs were used to deal with the increased power. The bump stops were moved from the body to the trailing arm itself, but the rebound stop continued to act on the arm of the damper. Somewhat surprisingly, the shock absorbers remained unchanged – and continued as standard specification for the TR6 although uprated dampers were available. The TR6 at first used the same coil springs as the TR5, but from CP 52868/CC 61571 these were uprated and the trailing wishbone arm support brackets were strengthened. Uprated springs meant a change in ride height and camber, so the brackets were changed by redesigning pivot and location holes to restore ride height and camber. In other respects, the IRS system continued virtually unchanged to the end of TR6 production.

Mention has been made in the 'Chassis' section of the solid axle TR4A offered in North America. This variant used a conventional TR4 axle suspended on equally conventional semi-elliptic springs. However, the TR4A's IRS chassis was used, with special brackets to carry the forward end of the springs. The rear of the springs rode on swinging shackles attached to the rear chassis cross-tube, which thus once again fulfilled a vital part of its original function. Lever arm shock absorbers were mounted as on the IRS TR4A, these acting via 90° drop links on the distance pieces which lived above the springs and which were clamped to them by the 'U' bolts.

Because the cars fitted with solid axle rear suspension were numbered in the normal TR4A commission number series (albeit with a TR4 'CT' rather than a 4A 'CTC' prefix), it has not been possible to establish how many were manufactured, but the number must run to several thousand. No such solid axle option was offered on the North American TR250 or carburettor TR6.

STEERING

The arrival of the TR4 saw a major advance in the steering system fitted to TR sports cars. For the first time, rack and pinion, manufactured by Alford & Alder, was used to endow the car with lighter and more accurate steering.

The rack was mounted behind the radiator and ran transversely above the chassis frame members, being attached by 'U' bolts to brackets welded to the top of the chassis. From the rack, ball-jointed track rod ends bolted to steering levers, which were in turn bolted to the vertical links forming part of the front suspension. Rubber bellows were wired in place at each end of the rack to exclude dust and retain lubricant, and track adjustment was effected by lock-nutted and threaded ends on the steering rack tie rods. The steering column, incorporating two flexible couplings, was in three basic pieces: an upper inner and upper outer column, together with a lower column which fed into the rack. Splined clamps and 'flats' on the column allowed for some measure of in/out adjustment, and there was a modicum of 'collapsible' crash protection compared with the earlier type of 'sidescreen' TR column.

Two types of rack were used on the TR4, the change taking place at CT 20064 (LHD) and CT 20266 (RHD). At this point, the previous solid aluminium block mountings were changed to rubber bushes, and the steering arms and chassis mounts differed. However, the rack used on the TR4A was common to TR5s and TR6s. As previously, the great majority of all these TRs were built with left-hand steering.

The steering required only 2½ turns from lock to lock on the earlier TR4s and the turning circle was quoted at 33ft in both directions. A 16in Bluemels black plastic wheel with wire spokes was fitted, the spokes each consisting of four wires disposed in a 'T' shape. The central horn push usually, but not always, carred a Triumph shield badge. A moderately retrograde step on the TR4A (and also apparently on late TR4s) was that the number of turns from lock to lock was increased to 3½, presumably to lighten steering effort further. The turning circle remained at 33ft, and a similar

16in steering wheel to the TR4s was fitted.

For the TR5 and TR6, the number of turns from lock to lock was reduced to 3¼. As the rack was the same as the TR4A's, presumably the lock-stop settings were slightly altered to take account of the wider wheels now being fitted. Turning circle was unaltered on the TR5, but on the TR6 it was quoted at 34¾ft left and 35½ft right. The TR5 was given a new 15in steering wheel design, with the spokes and rim covered with foam-filled matt black material, vinyl for the spokes and leather for the rim, to give a more modern appearance. The Triumph badge horn push centre was still used.

Upon introduction, the TR6 had a black 15in steering wheel with non-padded spokes, each spoke having holes of increasing diameter towards the centre. The Triumph shield was retained. This type of wheel was short-lived; cars from the 1970 model year (CP 50001 onwards) had a wheel with a silver anodised finish and spokes with slots, not holes. Early in 1971, a steering column lock was introduced to home-market TR6s at CP 52786, although LHD cars had had this feature from CP 50001. With the arrival of the 'CR' series TR6s at the end of 1972, the steering wheel was changed yet again. Of 14½in diameter, it had slightly thicker rim padding, the central boss padding being changed to fake stitching from the previous smooth finish, and the horn push finally dropped the Triumph shield and adopted white 'Triumph' lettering. Silver anodised slotted spokes in an approximate 'T' shape were still used.

On the TR4, front wheel toe-in was ⅛in, camber angle was 2°, castor angle was 3° and swivel pin inclination was 7°. The TR4A and TR5 had front wheel toe-in of 0 to 1/16in, camber angle of ½°, castor angle of 2¾° and swivel pin inclination of 8½°. The TR6 has the same toe-in, camber and castor values, but the swivel pin inclination was 9°.

BRAKES

The TR4 was introduced with a Girling hydraulic braking system similar to that used on the last TR3As. The Girling 'B' type split caliper assembly with 11in discs was kept for the front, while at the rear were similar Girling 9 × 1¾in drums. A total of 88½sq in of friction lining (28 sq in front and 60½ sq in rear) worked on a rubbed area of disc and drum combined of

346sq in. A mechanical handbrake as already described for the earlier TRs worked on the rear wheels, the lever being like the TR3A's and similarly positioned.

Early in 1962, from CT 4388 (disc wheels) and CT 4390 (wire wheels), completely different Girling front calipers of 16P type (as used on the TR3B) were introduced; pad size was reduced and the discs themselves slightly modified at the same time. The swept area of the new disc pads was now only 20.7sq in. Pads were changed again at CT 7630 (wire wheels) and CT 7747 (disc wheels). The only change to the TR4's rear brakes came at CT 5656 (wire wheels) and CT 5783 (disc wheels) when the bore of the master cylinder was reduced from .075in to .070in to soften the brake pedal following the introduction of the new calipers.

The TR4A used the front braking system – pads, discs and calipers – from late TR4s. The internals and dimensions of the rear brakes were also similar, but a different drum was used on the 4A owing to the hub changes necessitated by IRS. The TR4A's handbrake system (including that on the solid axle cars) was quite new – and as anyone who has had to stop on the handbrake will confirm, it is vastly inferior to the TR2/3/3A/4 type. One must presume that it was redesigned not only because of the arrival of IRS, but also to solve the old problem of which side of the transmission tunnel to put the lever, having regard to whether a car was left- or right-hand drive. The new handbrake lever, which sat on top of the tunnel, was not as long as the old one, and this, combined with the higher mounting position, ensured that much less 'pull' could be exerted. A fly-off action, as on the TR4, was retained, but this was deleted on the TR5/6. A fork-piece at the base of the lever pulled via a compensator onto twin cables, these each comprising an inner and an outer cable. These cables ran directly via fork-ends to the brake levers on the rear brake backplates, travelling on top of the spring-retaining chassis bridge-piece and along the rear trailing arms. This handbrake design continued through to the end of the TR6.

Although a brake servo was offered as an option for the TR4 and TR4A, it only became standard equipment on the TR5. It was a direct-acting servo which changed sides with the pedal box and the new tandem master cylinder for left- or right-hand drive. There was a modern, translucent plastic brake fluid reservoir with a large diameter cap, and the brake pedal and pedal box arrangement differed from the TR4A. The TR4A's discs and 16P calipers were considered adequate for the TR5 and TR6 with a servo added, and the rear brakes also continued unchanged on these models. During the TR6 run, the thread on the caliper assemblies was changed from imperial to metric at CP 76095 and CC 81079, but otherwise there were no significant modifications.

Pendant pedals, fitted with grip rubbers and acting directly on the master cylinder via a pedal box, were fitted to all these TRs. The stop lamps on all cars from late TR4s from CT 26931 onward were activated by a spring plunger switch operating directly on the brake pedal, whereas earlier TR4s had used a hydraulic pressure switch.

Brake drums on all cars were painted black, while calipers and master and slave cylinders were usually left as cast. The TR4 had a hydraulic pipe system very much as described for the TR3A, with two flexible hoses for the front wheels and a single one at the rear travelling from the chassis to the axle. All IRS cars had four flexible hoses, the rear brakes having one each, connected by a transverse pipe that crossed the chassis on the spring-retaining bridge piece. Extra rigid piping was necessary on the TR5 and TR6 to cope with the safety-inspired tandem master cylinder arrangement, the front and rear circuits being separated.

On North American specification TR250/TR6 models, a warning light was illuminated by a pressure differential sensor if one of the two circuits failed – but this seems not to have been fitted to cars for other markets. The rigid axle TR4A used three brake hoses – one for each front wheel and a single rear one from the chassis to the left-hand brake backplate. From here, a rigid pipe traversed the axle to actuate the other rear brake.

Rear Axle & Final Drive

Again, two entirely different systems were used. The TR4 and the rigid-axle TR4As had the conventional 'banjo' axle, differential and hub units that were fully described in the TR2/3/3A chapter. On the IRS cars, the differential and crown wheel and pinion housing was mounted on the chassis, with splined and jointed driveshafts driving the rear hubs and wheels.

The TR4 axle was 3in wider than the earlier item, this increase being achieved merely by lengthening the tubes and the halfshafts inside. The axles were painted

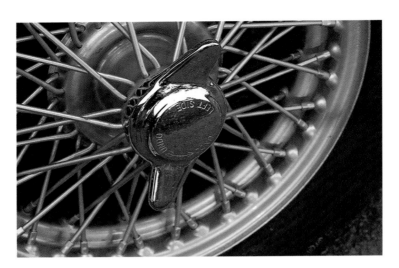

The Dunlop 60-spoke wire wheel was of 4½J section with double-butted spokes. This was the wheel supplied when TR4As were ordered with the wire wheel option. Note that the hub nut merely carries removal instructions, and not the maker's name.

black, and were individually numbered in a separate 'CT' series. Oil capacity remained at 1½ pints, and the 3.7 to 1 and 4.1 to 1 alternative ratios remained available as before. Having by the early 1960s refined the axle to an excellent state of reliability, Triumph needed to make no modifications other than a minor change in the thrust washer arrangement at axle number CT 33066.

The IRS cars continued with the same basic differential and crown wheel and pinion assembly, and on the TR4A the same two ratios were offered. The TR5 and TR6 had a 3.45 to 1 ratio, on both overdrive and non-overdrive cars, but the less powerful TR250 and carburettor TR6 for the USA continued to use the original 3.7 to 1 ratio. The IRS type differential housing, still painted black, had mounting plates bolted to it front and rear, and on the TR4A these each carried two rubber mounted fixings to the chassis. The more powerful, later cars had a different rear housing cover incorporating four rear mounting points, making six in all. The drive emerged from each side of the housing via short stub axles to drive flanges, to which were bolted driveshafts with universal joints at each end. The outer universal joint formed part of a further short driveshaft, which was journalled in a hub carrier housing bolted to the rear trailing arm. A key in the tapered driveshaft engaged with the slot and taper of the rear drive flange and hub itself. The whole rear drive unit contained so many parts, some of which needed special tools to service, that it is not surprising that manufacturing costs increased considerably. However, the Triumph engineers, one presumes, did a thorough job when devising the IRS, as the parts catalogues show very few modifications in production. The wire

wheel option, which continued to be available to 1973, necessitated hub extensions to the drive flanges.

The TR4's propshaft was marginally shorter than the TR3A's, to allow for the slightly greater length of the all-synchromesh gearbox. As previously, it was manufactured by Hardy-Spicer and painted black. Although the TR4A has two different propshafts listed (one carries the same part number as the TR4 type), I suspect that both types are in fact the same, the two part numbers merely indicating different manufacturers. The propshaft continued for the TR5 and TR6 without change, although the grease nipple was deleted in the TR6 application in respect of one of the shafts listed.

The TR6 parts catalogues list 4.1:1, 4.3:1, 4.55:1, and 4.875:1 ratios as being available for competition purposes. The standard 3.45:1 ratio of the petrol-injection cars gave the following overall gear ratios: first, 10.8:1; second, 6.92:1; third, 4.59:1; top, 3.45:1; overdrive, 2.82:1; reverse, 11.11:1. Road speeds with standard 165-section tyres are 21.2mph per 1000rpm in top and 25.9mph per 1000rpm in overdrive top. When the 'J' type overdrive replaced the 'A' type in the TR6 in 1973, road speeds became 21.8mph and 26.6mph per 1000rpm respectively.

Wheels & Tyres

The TR4 and TR4A both used the same 4½J disc road wheels, chromed nave plates and 'globe' medallions as the earlier cars. As usual, a knock-off wire-wheel option was available. Early TR4 customers received only 48-spoke wires with 4in rims, which were barely adequate in strength for the increased weight of the car; 60-spoke wheels with 4½in rims could be obtained to special order, and it would be unwise today to use original 48-spoke wheels on TR4s other than for gentle motoring or 'show originality' purposes. During the TR4's run, the 60-spoke wheels eventually became the norm when wire wheels were specified, and these continued for the TR4A and TR5. On the TR4 and TR4A, chromed knock-off nuts were fitted to the wire wheels, but octagonal safety nuts were available for certain export markets (notably Germany) as early as 1962.

Disc wheels continued to be finished in the silver lacquer/aluminium wheel paint described in the TR2/3/3A chapter. Wire wheels came in aluminium, silver lacquer, dull or bright chrome to order.

The TR5 received wider 5in disc wheels, although some contemporary sources still referred to 4½in rims. Additionally, fake Rostyle finishers were added, of a type fashionable in the late 1960s. The Rostyle finisher was in matt black and stainless steel with five 'spokes' and five embossed 'wheel nuts'. Wire wheels for the TR5 remained the TR4/4A 60-spoke type, still of 4½in rim width, but are believed to have come with octagonal nuts as standard. According to the parts book, the dull chrome and silver lacquer finishes were no longer available. This book also refers to a 6in cast alloy wheel; if these existed at all they must be very rare, as I have never seen a car so fitted.

A further increase in rim width was provided for TR6 disc wheels, which were 5½in wide. For the 1969 model year TR6s, TR5-type Rostyle trims were fitted, with slightly extended 'pips' to hold the nave plate. From CP 50001, a new disc wheel design was introduced, with 15 instead of 12 radial cooling holes and a matt black hub trim that left the four wheel nuts – now domed and chromium plated – exposed. The nave plate holding 'pips' were deleted, while in the centre of the hub trim was a red badge with 'TR6' written in white. Upon the introduction of the CR series TR6s at the end of 1972, the hub centre trims on the disc wheels changed from matt black to a satin silver finish. Many later American specification TR6s had deep rim embellishers fitted, made from highly polished, brushed aluminium.

A wire wheel option – a stronger 5½in rim with 72 spokes – remained for the TR6 until May 1973, but it became increasingly less popular during the car's production

The Rostyle wheel cover – standard on disc-wheeled TR5s, TR250s and early TR6s – complete with dummy wheel nuts. These red band tyres, fashionable in 1968, were original factory equipment, made by Michelin or Goodyear. There is a red side marker light below the TR250 badge.

Most CP series TR6s had this type of disc wheel (wires were still then an option) with a black central insert. However, 1969 model cars had TR5 type Rostyle wheel trims.

The CR/CF series TR6s had wheels with satin silver centres, rather than the previous black. On these later wheels the rim was welded to the centre all round rather than at specific points. All wheel centre badges are red. The chromed beading around the base of the hardtop can also be seen.

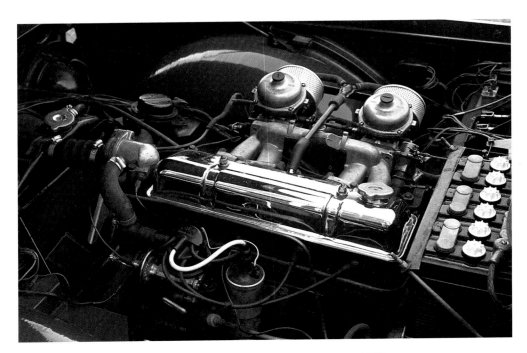

The engine bay of a late TR4 showing the later radiator without the backwards-facing TR3A type header tank. The battery is of the correct type for the period, with individual fillers for each cell and external strapping. The white HT lead is an incorrect colour.

The same engine from the other side shows the Stromberg 175CD carburettors and the improved inlet manifold. Also visible is the later type of oil filler cap and later air filters with recirculatory breathing system. The air horn trumpets which can just be seen are not original.

run. Wire wheels were zinc-plated as standard or chromed at extra cost, and octagonal safety nuts were provided.

The TR4 came as standard on the 5-90×15 crossply Dunlops that had been supplied for TR3As. Dunlop RS5 high-speed tyres, Michelin 'X' radials and Goodyear white-wall tyres were optional extras. Later in the run, Goodyear 'Motorway Special' tyres were also offered – and occasional supply problems led to other brands being used. The TR4A was introduced with crossply tyres as standard, often Goodyear Grand Prix, but it seems that most cars were actually delivered on radials of various types, at least for the home market. The crossply tyres were initially listed as 5-90×15 size, but an early sales brochure refers to the size as 6-95×15. Dunlop SP41

and Michelin 'X' radials of 165-section were again available at extra cost. By 1967, when the TR5 was introduced, the radial ply tyre had virtually vanquished the cross-ply, at least as far as high-performance cars were concerned. As far as I can ascertain, all TR5s, whether on disc or wire wheels, were delivered on 165-section radial tyres, either Dunlop SP41s or Michelins of the then-new and revolutionary asymmetrical XAS type.

The original tyres specified for the TR6 were 165 HR 15 radials, usually Goodyear, Dunlop or Michelin XAS. The same tyre was used on wire or steel wheels. By 1972, but possibly earlier, 185-section tyres were being fitted to cars destined for North America, and these must have served slightly to increase the overall gearing. It is

believed that some home market cars went out on 175-section Michelin XAS tyres, and later in the production run 185-section tyres were fitted to some non-North American cars.

The TR4 kept the TR3A-type screw pillar jack that engaged with lugs on the chassis, together with similar wheel changing tools. The standard tool kit was quoted as comprising 'set of AF spanners, set of feeler gauges, grease gun, screwdriver, wheelbrace, valve core key, grips or pliers, adjustable spanner, plug spanner, tommy-bar and nave plate remover'. In addition, a copper-faced hammer was provided with the wire wheel option.

The TR4A, TR5 and TR6 used a screw-scissors type jack, which was worked by a hooked, bent wire handle and could be placed anywhere under the chassis. The chassis lugs were not present on the new IRS chassis. Autocar's TR4A road test, incidentally, commented on how efficiently and quickly this new jack could be used. By the time of the TR5 and TR6, the tool kit had become somewhat depleted, consisting of a plug spanner and tommy-bar, a box spanner, three open-ended spanners, feeler gauge and the wheel changing tools appropriate to the type of wheels fitted (an octagonal spanner was provided for 'safety' wire wheel nuts).

ENGINE

The TR4 and TR4A used the classic Standard Vanguard wet-liner engine in 86mm bore form, giving a capacity of 2138cc (the 1991cc engine was available to special order for the TR4 but probably not for the TR4A). Since this engine, fully described in the previous chapter, reached a plateau of development and reliability in the TR3A, very little needed to be done to it for the TR4/4A series.

A new engine front plate was fitted as the mounting points on these cars are further

Two under bonnet views of the TR5. The direct-acting, in-line brake servo operated twin circuit brakes, for the first time on a TR. The correct 15AC alternator is seen, with an external regulator. An oil cooler is fitted to this car as an accessory, and an additional oil feed to the rocker gear has been added – this is a good idea, although not original. The oil filler cap should be silver/grey, but a chromed rocker box is original on TR5s and early TR6s. This car is fitted with the later-type air bleed – the earlier type had a brass fitting on the inlet manifold. The servo hose is not routed correctly, and the air inlet tubes are not original in that they are not the moulded type. Original throttle cables were green, rather than blue. The bonnet catch assembly could be either painted body colour or, more usually, zinc-plated.

apart, but if the correct plate is used there is no reason why a 'sidescreen' TR engine will not fit a TR4/4A, and *vice versa*. Certain carburation and manifolding changes were made and will be dealt with later, but for the TR4 there was no major modification (other than cubic capacity) to the TR3A/B engine.

Compression ratio increased from 8.5:1 to 9:1 as a simple function of the capacity increase, and this, coupled with the extra 147cc, meant that maximum power increased by 5 per cent, from 100bhp gross to 105bhp gross (or 100bhp net) and maximum torque increased by 8 per cent to 127lb ft. Camshaft timing was slightly changed, to 17°/57°/57°/17°. All this was ample to ensure that performance was maintained, despite the new bodyshell's extra weight. A starting handle dog was still fitted to the crankshaft nose of the TR4 engine, but the handle itself was available only as an optional extra; this item was deleted on the TR4A.

From engine number CT 21471 E, a modified cylinder head assembly was fitted to the TR4, and at CT 14234 E the first signs of impending US restrictions manifested themselves when the previous open-circuit combined engine breather/oil filler cap was replaced by a closed-circuit type. The rocker cover, which was chromed, had the oil filler/breather at the bulkhead end, whereas the TR3A's was at the radiator end. The open-circuit breather was painted black with a 'recommended oils' transfer in

white, whereas the later TR4A oil filler cap looked more like a radiator cap, painted silver and incorporating a metered valve which allowed air to be sucked in. TR4/4A engine mounting rubber bushes were circular in outline, whereas those for 'sidescreen' cars were oblong. The full-flow oil filter was now by Automotive Products or Tecalamit rather than Purolator.

The TR4A had a new design of camshaft with a revised profile to match the improved inlet and exhaust manifolds, and power output improved slightly to 104bhp net. Crankcase breathing became a fully closed-circuit system, and a Smiths 'Anti Smog' valve was incorporated into the breathing arrangements. Late TR4s with the closed-circuit breathing and all TR4As also dispensed with wire mesh air filters,

having instead twin paper element filters, painted silver, with an oval drum-type shape. As before, the four-cylinder engines and principal ancillaries were painted black or left as cast.

By the mid-1960s, it was obvious to Triumph that a major increase in power output would be needed to ensure that the TR's healthy sales record continued. Following two false starts – the first with the expensive twin-cam 'Sabrina' engine and the second with a 'stretched' 2½-litre version of the existing engine with 'dry' cylinder liners – the decision was taken to develop a more reliably powerful version of the company's six-cylinder 2-litre engine which had already been used in tuned form in the works rally Triumph 2000 saloons. This six-cylinder engine had first been used

The immaculate engine bay of Eric Barrett's TR6. Originality is perfect apart from these points: the chromed rocker cover is only correct on 1969 model cars; the flame trap should be grey, not red; the cooling system expansion bottle should have a black top; and the battery retaining bar should be black.

in the Standard Vanguard 'Vignale' Six of 1959/60 and was later fitted to the production Triumph 2000. Its origins lay in the Standard '8' four-cylinder economy saloon of 1953: by progressively stretching the bore size, adding two cylinders and finally increasing the stroke, what had started as a 26bhp 803cc engine became a 150bhp 2498cc unit!

Unlike the wet-liner TR2-4A engine, the TR5/6 engine was dry-linered and of very conventional construction. Both block and head were of cast iron, a new design of 12-port head being developed specially for the TR application. The crankshaft ran in four main bearings and the camshaft was driven by duplex chain from the crankshaft nose. The Lucas 22D6 distributor, fuel metering unit and oil pump were propelled by a skew gear driven shaft from the camshaft, while the water pump and alternator were belt driven from the crankshaft, which itself carried the plastic fan on an extension piece. Flat-top aluminium alloy pistons were fitted, each with two compression rings and two scraper rings, the latter separated by a spacer. Conventional rocker gear and the 12 overhead valves were driven by tappets and upright pushrods, double valve springs being fitted. The AC full-flow oil filter system was mounted directly onto the right-hand side of the block, below the distributor.

The fuel-injection car's compression ratio was 9.5:1, but 8.6:1 was used for the carburettor version. Bore and stroke were 74.7mm × 95.0mm respectively, tappet clearance was .010in both for inlet and exhaust valves, and fuel injection allowed valve timing that was verging on the wild at 35°/65°/65°/35°. The resultant power output was quoted as 150bhp net and maximum torque of 164lb ft occurred at 3000rpm. The carburettor TR250 suffered considerably, with maximum power of 104bhp net (the same as the TR4A) and peak torque of 143lb ft at 3500rpm. A milder camshaft was fitted, timed at 10°/50°/50°/10°.

This engine was modified only in minor detail during the 15-month production run of the TR5/250 and was virtually unchanged for early TR6s. As is well-known, difficulties in keeping the injected engines in tune, a desire to improve emission characteristics and general customer complaints all forced Triumph to detune the fuel-injected engine at the end of 1972, at the introduction of the 'CR' series cars. The camshaft was replaced by a much milder 18°/58°/58°/18° item, although the compression ratio stayed at 9.5:1. The result was a better-tempered but slower car, 124bhp at the then-new 'DIN' measurement being quoted.

Carburettor TR6s initially used the TR250 engine, but in late 1970 the 18°/58°/58°/18° camshaft was introduced, together with a reduction in compression ratio to 7.75:1. Compression ratio was further reduced to 7.5:1 in late 1974. These 'federalised' North American cars also suffered from an exhaust gas recirculation system, and finally an air injection pump was added to further clean up the exhaust.

On injected engines, the block fitting for a camshaft-operated fuel pump was blanked off, but this was used on carburettor cars for an AC mechanical pump. These latter cars had a conventional air cleaner system consisting of a single elongated oval canister containing two disposable elements, the canister, painted silver, being bolted direct to the carburettors. The injected cars had a drum-type filter mounted to one side of the radiator, this feeding into a cylindrical gallery which in turn fed the inlet manifold via six wire-clipped flexible hoses.

Engine blocks were usually painted black with silver-painted rocker covers, although these have often been subsequently chromed; TR5s, TR250s and 1969 model year TR6s had chromed covers as standard. Most ancillaries were left in the colours as supplied by their manufacturers; the air collection gallery cylinder was painted matt silver, whereas the air cleaner drum was black.

COOLING SYSTEM

The TR4 was introduced with a radiator block very similar in type to the TR2/3/3A item. Even the starting handle hole remained, but the handle itself was an optional extra. The backwards-extending

A yellow fan, with seven or eight blades, was fitted to the TR5. The black, drum-type air cleaner is correct, but this radiator, as is common, seems to have lost its shrouding.

CR/CF TR6s are correctly fitted with a 13-blade fan in red plastic.

header tank and filler was still included, even though no longer strictly required by the new body design. The radiator was secured by stays to the chassis front upper cross-member. From CT9553, a modified radiator was fitted, with the header tank and filler now incorporated in the top of the radiator itself. A ducting shroud made of composition material was fitted in front of the radiator to force air along the correct path.

Conventional water pump circulation was used, a four-blade fan was fitted on the crankshaft nose, and a by-pass route and thermostat were employed. The system was pressurised at 4psi (later TR4s and all TR4As were at 7psi) and the water capacity was 14 pints (including heater). An 82 degree thermostat was normal for the home market but 88 degree items were also fitted, while other differently rated thermostats were used to suit local export conditions. A brass radiator drain tap was fitted, together with a block drain tap. Normal running temperature, as before, was 185 degrees F. As previously, the fan was balanced, and acted with its extension piece as a vibration damper for the crankshaft. Radiator blocks and bracketry should be painted black, fan blades were painted aluminium colour with black steelwork, and the thermostat housing was left as cast.

The TR4 incorporated for the first time a Smiths fresh air heater, rated at 2.5 kw. This unit was fed by a vent on top of the scuttle and it sat behind the dashboard below this point. A fan blower motor was fitted. Unlike the earlier cars, all controls, including the hot water valve, could be operated from the driver's seat. The heater unit and ducting should be painted black. Demisting vents were incorporated, air flow to these or to the cockpit area being controlled by a dashboard knob.

The TR4A had a different radiator block which was wider than either of the TR4 types. Water capacity was reduced to 11 pints with heater, and the starting handle hole in the radiator finally disappeared, for the option had been deleted. A 'no-loss' arrangement for the TR4A consisted of a plastic pipe from the filler neck leading into a bottle mounted low down at the side of the radiator.

Home market TR4As used the same fan as the TR4s, but a six-blade fan was fitted for cars exported to hotter climates. The TR4A parts manual also refers to a plastic fan, but no introductory point is given. Both TR4s and TR4As had their water pumps and dynamos driven by the same large section 'V' belt that had been used on the 'sidescreen' cars.

On the six-cylinder cars, the general layout and principles of the cooling system were similar, but the TR5 had an uprated radiator, even though it was outwardly similar to the TR4A item. The TR6 fielded three different radiators, again looking similar: one was for US specification cars, the second was an early non-US type that was the same as the TR5's, and the third was the non-US type

This rear view of the TR6 hardtop also shows the later type of fuel filler cap. This was a 'safety' item which could not spring open in the event of the car overturning, unlike the earlier one with the release 'tongue'.

used following the change from the TR5 type. The overflow bottle system was retained for TR5s and TR6s. The thermostat housing was now bolted to the top of the water pump, the thermostat itself now being fitted vertically rather than horizontally. The water pump was again belt driven, now by a more modern, thinner section 'V' belt, and was bolted to the front face of the cylinder head rather than to the block.

An eight-blade plastic fan, bolted as usual to the front of the crankshaft via an extension piece, was used on the TR5 and TR6s up to engine number CP 52420, but a seven-blade fan was used for the remainder of the 'CP' series run and a 13-blade fan for the 'CR' series. The TR4A's Smiths heater unit continued virtually unchanged for the TR5s and TR6s, although additional vents for warming the feet and knees were incorporated. The six-cylinder cooling system was pressurised at 7psi in the later TR5/250, although the manual states that radiators on early cars were still rated at 4psi. The TR6 carried a more modern high-pressure system set at 13psi – experience has shown that 13psi suits all the six-cylinder TRs. Thermostat specification remained at 88 degrees (cold climate) and 82 degrees ('normal' climate, whatever that was). Norma running temperature remained at 185 degrees F and water capacity was 11 pints including the heater.

This fuel filler was similar on TR4/4A/5 and early TR6 models, and virtually indistinguishable from the TR3A item. The release tongue should point to the driver's side of the car.

EXHAUST SYSTEM

The TR4 used a slightly modified version of the TR3A/B exhaust system, the manifold, main silencer and auxiliary silencer and combined tailpipe all continuing unchanged. Only the bracketry and hangings were adapted to fit the TR4's chassis.

The TR4A had a more efficient cast exhaust manifold with four branches that became two – rather than one – at the flange joint with the twin front pipes. Thus the gases from the inner and outer exhaust ports remained separate until they entered the front silencer box, in which they mingled to exit through a single pipe. In turn this pipe gave into an elongated 'Y' shaped section with two exits, feeding into a pair of oval-shaped rear silencer boxes,

each of which had an integral upswept tail pipe and a built-in hanger bracket. The twin tail pipes emerged under the rear bumper quite close together in the centre of the car.

This system, with its three silencers, was not wholly satisfactory in use, as well as being costly to manufacture and replace. It certainly gave low noise levels, but did nothing for the gas-flow characteristics. Consequently, the system was redesigned quite early in the TR4A's production run. The front silencer was deleted and a 'Y' piece joining the two separate downpipes was substituted. A cranked single pipe then carried the gases to the rear of the car into a large, single, oval, transverse silencer box with an integral tail pipe which exited on the nearside. This system was fixed as usual at the rear engine mounting, and the trans-

A nice shot of a clean but 'used' engine bay. As is correct for a late TR4A, the carburettors are SU HS6 types. The fuel feed pipes were originally just 'push-fit', but most owners prefer to clip them for safety. The air horns and relay are accessories. The radiator appears to have lost its air ducting, which can lead to overheating.

verse silencer had both forward and aft flexible hangings from the chassis. Although slightly noisier, this modified exhaust was still quieter than the TR4 type and rather more efficient.

A system similar to this later TR4A type was used for the TR5, but here twin pipes were used throughout, the single transverse silencer box having twin inlets and outlets. The cast exhaust manifold was a four-branch type, two of the branches being formed of pairs of pipes to cater for the six exhaust ports. This manifold fed into a flanged joint which connected into the twin downpipes. The same exhaust manifold was used for all fuel-jected TR6s and later carburettor TR6s, but earlier carburettor TR6s (up to engine number CC 75000) and TR250s had a manifold with only one exit and a single front and intermediate pipe. The transverse silencer in this case had one inlet but still had two integral tail pipes, whereas later carburettor cars and all injection TR6s had a 'twin throughout' system very similar to the TR5's. The parts books indicate several alternative silencer specifications for different export markets, notably France, Germany and Switzerland.

Exhaust manifolds were left as cast, but pipes, brackets and silencers on all cars were finished in black or silver.

CARBURETTORS & FUEL INJECTION

The TR4 started its production run with the traditional twin SU set-up, keeping the TR3A's 1¾in H6 carburettors with brass dashpot caps and wire mesh air cleaners. However, push-on type rubber connectors were now used in the fuel pipe runs and no fuel shut-off tap was fitted. The black-painted fuel tank, of 11¾ gallons capacity, was sited in roughly the same lateral position under the rear bulkhead as on the earlier cars. A rubber pipe projected upwards from the top of the tank towards the rear deck panel to connect with the traditional TR snap-action filler cap. The tank was vented at the top by a separate vent pipe attached via a banjo connection. The standard carburettor needles were SU type SM, no change having been necessary with the increased engine capacity. Fuel continued to be pumped by a camshaft-driven AC pump.

The use of 1¾in SUs continued until engine number CT 16800 E, at which point a trial run of 100 cars were produced with Stromberg type 175CD 1¾in constant vacuum carburettors. It seems that Triumph wanted to fit this carburettor, based on the SU principle, purely because it was manufactured by an independent concern, and not, as with the SU, by its arch-rival, the British Motor Corporation! Although a redesigned and improved inlet manifold was introduced with these carburettors, the attachment points remained identical, so either type of carburettor fits either manifold. The manifold incorporated a take-off in connection with the closed-circuit breathing system. For some

reason, possibly contractural, a complete changeover to Strombergs did not take place for a further few months, but from engine number CT 21471 E all TR4s had the new carburettors and manifold as standard.

Strombergs were used well into the TR4A's production run, but at commission number CT 62191 SUs became standard again, still on the improved manifold. This change may well have been prompted because the formation of the British Leyland Motor Corporation meant that SUs were no longer supplied by a rival, but were now manufactured within the group of which Triumph had become a part. The SUs were now the updated HS6 type, with black plastic dashpot caps and improved petrol feed arrangements between the float chambers and the carburettor bodies. The standard needle changed to type TW. The paper element air filters continued from the Strombergs on to the SUs, and the parts catalogue lists an additional 'air cleaner and silencer' assembly, stated to be to special order only. In this, the air filters were enclosed in an elongated oval box, but how many cars were actually fitted with this remains uncertain. The fuel system on the TR4A otherwise remained similar to the TR4 type, except for pipework, clip and throttle linkage changes which had become necessary because of the carburettor and manifold substitutions.

Upon its introduction in 1967, the TR5 became the first British series production car to be fitted with fuel injection. This

Two under-bonnet views of a CP series TR6 showing the commission plate on the wheel arch and the eight-blade yellow plastic fan. Some top hoses were originally supplied in this peculiar green colour, but the red overflow bottle hose should be clear plastic. Note also the correctly painted rocker cover. On a TR6 of this age (1970), a 'fir-tree' connector is incorrect for the injection leads – CP cars had a rubber strap arrangement.

development allowed the use of a camshaft with a more advanced profile than would otherwise have been possible, so that power output grew sufficiently for the TR to remain competitive in performance terms. Triumph wished to use a British injection system and only Lucas was offering anything ready for production – but development continued in the hands of the first customers!

The heart of the system was the shuttle-type fuel metering unit, driven by gearing from the distributor drive shaft and bolted to the left-hand side of the engine between the distributor and the bulkhead. This unit received petrol at high pressure from the tank via a fuel filter assembly and a specially developed Lucas fuel pump. This was electrically powered for the first time on a TR,

and initially the pump was sited in the engine compartment. However, excessive heat in this position soon caused problems with vaporisation, so the pump was quickly repositioned in the boot. Nevertheless, vaporisation problems have persisted ever since in hot weather, despite the addition of cooling coils to the pump and other modifications.

From the mechanical metering unit, fuel was fed via six plastic pipes to the individual injectors, which were screwed into the inlet manifolds. There were three of these manifolds, each having two ports to give an individual entry passage for each cylinder. Air was introduced to each cylinder via six flexible pipes connected to the manifolds from the air collection reservoir cylinder previously described. Fuel was pumped

constantly at a consistent pressure from the tank, there being a return pipe system so that fuel not required by the engine at any given moment was returned to the tank for re-circulation. A cold start knob was fitted, which opened the throttles and caused the metering unit to deliver a richer mixture. Throttle control was achieved by a cable, bell crank and countershaft arrangement. Apart from the pump changing position, this new fuel system ran through the short life of the TR5 with little modification.

Due to increasingly severe exhaust emission regulations then becoming enforced in the USA, cars for North America were not sold with the fuel injection system, which, somewhat surprisingly, could not be made to meet the requirements. As a result, the TR250 was produced, these cars having the new six-cylinder engine with twin emission-controlled Stromberg 175 CD carburettors which could, by careful tuning, be made to meet the new regulations. The bad news was that power output at 104bhp net was no higher than the TR4A's, although torque was improved at 143 lb ft. The good news was that the cost of this carburettor system was very much lower.

A new '2 into 6' one-piece inlet manifold was developed, water-heated by a pipe from the water pump. An AC mechanical fuel pump was used, with just a single fuel line from the tank and a small plastic in-line fuel filter. The fuel tank itself was very similar to the TR4A type, but all three tanks for the TR4A/5/250 differed in detail. Quoted

TR250 under-bonnet view shows the six-cylinder engine with Stromberg carburettors and an elongated oval air cleaner box. The direct-acting brake servo and cooling system expansion bottle are visible, and the alternator is by now standard equipment. The commission plate's new home is on the front wheelarch.

capacities differ depending upon which source one believes – 11¼, 11½ and 11¾ gallons are all mentioned.

The TR6 injection cars continued to use the TR5 fuel system largely unchanged, although the fuel tank differed slightly from the start and was again modified at CP50001 to stop fuel surge, which was causing problems with the engine cutting out. The air intake manifold was also modified at CP50001, although the air cleaner assembly and element remained the same throughout. At least four fuel metering pumps, differing in detail, were used on the TR6, and a special 'high altitude' metering unit was available on cars for certain markets. Injectors remained the same as for the TR5. From the introduction of the 'CR' series TR6s, the fuel pipe assemblies, clips and elbows were changed, but the fuel pump itself remained unaltered from the TR5. The fuel filter continued to use the same element, but the filter unit itself differed slightly from the TR5 one. The later TR6 injection system incorporated an inertia switch to cut off the fuel supply in severe impact. Three different TR6 fuel filler caps are listed, one of which is the TR5 type, which in turn differed from the TR4/4A type – but the records do not reveal which type was fitted when.

The TR6 carburettor cars again used the constant-vacuum, emission-controlled Strombergs with a single fuel line and engine-driven AC pump. Four inlet manifolds differing in detail were fitted: up to en-gine number CC50000E, from CC50001E to CC75000E, from CC75001E to CF1, and from CF1 onwards. From CC50001E, a petrol vapour absorption device was fitted in addition to the emission-control system. The carburettor assemblies changed in detail several times, change points being given as up to CC50000E, from CC50001E to CC65346E, from CC65347E to CF 1 E, and from CF 1 E onwards – unfortunately there are too many detail changes to be elaborated here.

The great majority of TR6s built were carburettor cars, and these in fact stayed in production for the US market for more than a year after the final injected cars were built in February 1975. The last carburettor cars were built in July 1976, exactly 23 years after the first production TR2s were made.

TRANSMISSION

TR gearboxes remained remarkably un altered for many years. The unit introduced with the TR4 and 'TCF' TR3Bs was a development of the previous TR gearbox, differing principally in having syn-chromesh on first gear. As a result, the gearbox casing was ½in longer to accom-modate the extra synchro cone. Although the TR2/3/3A and TR3B/4 gearboxes are interchangeable with a little persuasion, the internals of the TR4 unit differed considera-bly and were sufficiently strong to cope with the 50 per cent power increase of the six-cylinder engines. The general layout and details of the gearbox have been described in the TR2/3/3A chapter.

The linkage was slightly redesigned in an attempt to eliminate sloppiness, but it had the unfortunate effect of making the TR4's – and subsequent models' – gearchange notably more notchy than those of earlier cars. The three upper ratios in this new gearbox were similar to those of the TR2/3/3A unit, but first and reverse gearing was higher, giving the following internal ratios: first, 3.14; second, 2.01; second o/d, 1.65; third, 1.33; third o/d, 1.09; top, 1.0; top o/d, 0.82; reverse, 3.22.

This gearbox was used with only very minor modification from the TR4 of 1961 through to the early TR6s of 10 years later. The parts catalogues quote three types of gearbox and clutch housing assemblies for the TR4: up to CT 31506 (31636 over-drive), from CT31507 (31637 overdrive) to CT50124, and from CT50125 onwards. The differences are minor, however, and interchangeability is evidently not affected. Again, different part numbers are quoted for the gear levers on each model, but the chromed levers appear largely similar although the knobs differ. The TR4/4A has a round black plastic knob with the gate pattern cut in white, whereas standard fit for the TR5 and TR6 was a somewhat pear-shaped, fabric-trimmed item – but some TR5s appear to have had a pear-shaped black plastic knob. The design of the TR6 knob changed slightly at CP 53854.

In mid-1971, the gearbox was finally altered in substance when it received redesigned and uprated internals, developed from the stronger Triumph Stag unit. The gearbox numbers involved were CP 51163 or CC 89817 onwards. The internal ratios changed slightly, to: first, 2.99; second, 2.10; third, 1.39; top, 1.0; reverse, 3.37. The revised overall ratios, therefore, were: first, 10.33; second, 7.25; third, 4.78; top, 3.45; reverse, 11.62.

A second change to transmission specification occurred almost at the beginning of the 1973 model year, when the old Laycock 'A' type overdrive unit (giving a step-up ratio of 0.82:1) was finally phased out after 20 years. This change came in just after the introduction of the CR series cars, probably at CR567, although I have not been able to establish this change point for certain. However, it appears always to have been fitted to the US-bound 'CF' cars. Although Laycock's 'J' type unit was more modern in design, it had the considerable disadvantage that it did not operate on second gear, bringing to an end the TR's unique seven-speed transmission system. The step-up ratio of this later unit was 0.797:1, so the overall gear ratio in overdrive top became 2.75:1 (based on a 3.45:1 differential), giving a road speed with standard wheels and tyres of 26.6mph per 1000rpm. With the US specification 3.7:1 differential and the 'J' type overdrive, the overall ratio of 2.95:1 gave 26.1mph per 1000rpm. Finally, after 20 years in the options list, overdrive began to be a standard fitment, it is thought from the start of the 1974 model year.

Gearboxes and overdrive units, as previously, were finished in silver/aluminium paint or left as cast. Propshafts, which again did not differ between overdrive and non-overdrive applications, were painted black.

The clutch came in for modification upon the introduction of the TR4A. The TR4 continued to use the Borg & Beck spring-type single dry-plate 9in clutch, hydraulically operated. However, in the interests of a lighter pedal operation, the TR4A was introduced with a diaphragm spring clutch, again by Borg & Beck, but the diameter was reduced slightly to 8½in. This seems to have been a retrograde step, as more than one contemporary road test commented that clutch slip was all too easy to provoke, something to which the old spring clutch was not prone. The diaphragm clutch was self-adjusting for wear, unlike the previous type.

The 8½in diameter plate remained for the TR5s and TR6s, but the diaphragm spring was strengthened to cope with the increased power. Correspondingly, to compensate for the increased pedal weight this would otherwise have produced, the clutch hydraulics were uprated, the system including a larger diameter slave cylinder. Some TR5 and TR6 clutches were of Laycock manufacture, not Borg & Beck. It should be noted that Borg & Beck and Laycock clutch plates and covers must be fitted in sets (a Laycock plate will not fit a Borg & Beck cover, and *vice versa*), a fact which has caused grief to unwitting TR owners over the years.

ELECTRICAL EQUIPMENT & LAMPS

Electrical parts continued to be supplied almost exclusively by Lucas. In all cars, from TR4 to TR6, the 12v battery inhabited the space aft of the engine, centrally positioned under the bonnet and on a shelf forming part of the front bulkhead. On TR4s and TR4As, a 57 AH battery of type BT9A was fitted; this was changed to type C9 on TR5s and early TR6s (CZ11/9 for cold climates), and to type P130 (AZ11 and AZ13 for export and cold climate) on later TR6s. The battery was clamped into placed by a right-angled bar, painted black and held by screwed hook-ended rods at either side to metal plates forming part of the bulkhead. The plastic colour-coded wiring loom had push-on connectors.

TR4s and almost all TR4As were fitted with dynamos, type C40/1; although an alternator was offered as a TR4A option, it is uncertain how many such cars were delivered. TR4s were positive earth, TR4As negative earth. The regulator box, type RB106/2, was mounted on the offside front inner wing. TR5s had an alternator as standard, driven by a smaller section drive belt than had been used for the dynamo equipped cars. The type number was 15AC, still with a separate control box of type 4TR, but became 15ACR on early TR6s, this type now incorporating the control system within the alternator. On later TR6s, the alternator was uprated to 16ACR for most markets – and 17ACR and 18ACR in turn for North America (but some US cars had an AC Delco unit). A type 4FJ fuse carrier containing 35 amp fuses was fitted to the TR4 and TR4A, replaced by type 7FJ for the six-cylinder cars. The 4FJ type had two fitted fuses and two spares, whereas the 7FJ had four fitted fuses and two spares.

Ignition coils were type HA12 on all but the later TR6s, for which type 15C6 – a six volt coil used with a ballast resistor – was substituted. Four-cylinder distributors were type DM2P4 for earlier TR4s, with 25D4 being substituted on the later TR4s (from CT 17954) and all TR4As. Six-cylinder cars had a type 22D6 distributor, variously modified to suit local export conditions. Champion L87Y or Lodge CNY plugs were standard for TR4/4As, while TR5s and early TRs had Champion UN12Ys, and later TR6s had Champion N9Ys – all had a .025in gap. High tension leads were usually black, but other colours – particularly red and green – were seen on later cars. Right-angled black plastic plug connectors were usual on four-cylinder cars; although but six-cylinder cars usually had straight-type plug connectors, either type seems to be correct on TR5s and TR6s. Original equipment lead sets for TR5/6s, by Lucas or Ripaults, usually have dark green carbon leads and black plastic end caps.

The TR4 and TR4A continued to employ the M418G inertia drive type starter motor, painted black (or sometimes red). The TR5 also used type M418G but of pre-engaged design, although an M35G/1 inertia drive type was an alternative that was also used on the TR250. Early TR6s continued to use the M418G, but later cars (from CP 53637 and CC 63845) used the pre-engaged type 2M100 starter. The type 2ST starter solenoid used on the TR4 and TR4A was replaced on the TR5/6 by the 4ST type.

The TR4 was still fitted as standard with single-speed, self-parking windscreen wipers, these being driven by a Lucas PS7 motor (but type DR3A is also listed) mounted on the nearside front bulkhead top, accessible from under the bonnet. The optional two-speed wiper motor was type 58SA. The TR4A had two-speed wipers as standard, but the motor was different, type DR3A, and continued for the TR5; the TR6 motor was 14W. Many different types of wiper blades (usually 10 or 10½in) and arms were used on these cars, the original blades being of Trico manufacture. Because of the ventilation flap let into the scuttle top, one wiper arm was cranked in order to clear the flap when opened. This arrangement appears to have continued on later TR6s, even when the flap had been replaced by an air inlet grille. Chromed blades and arms were used on the TR4/4A/5; although TR250s and many earlier CP and CC series

A late TR4 rear light lens, showing the circular pattern on the top and bottom lenses – earlier cars had a vertical pattern.

The TR5 had reversing lights, one on each side, as standard. This car appears to have the early type rear light lenses. The aggressive twin exhaust pipes show clearly. Correct on the TR5/250 is the painted wing bead.

A detailed shot of the sidelight/flasher repeater unit introduced with the TR4A. The chromed bezel on the sidelight lens is slightly too deep: it is probably the item produced for Lotus, one of the few other manufacturers to use this type of light.

Detail of early TR6 light unit and rear quarters. The TR5 type marker lights have been deleted. The coach line has been added and is not original.

TR6s had satin-finished silver items, some chromed ones did appear. With the introduction of the CR/CF series cars, matt black wiper blades and arms were substituted to fall in with fashion. Although the TR4/4A had a manual screenwash arrangement, the six-cylinder cars had electric washers of Lucas type 5SJ; the spray nozzles were mounted on the bezels surrounding the wiper arm spindles.

Twin black-painted horns – a matched pair of high and low note horns – were fitted to all these cars. Lucas type 9H horns were more usual, but some horns were manufactured by Clear Hooters Ltd.

Headlamps on TR4s, as on the TR3A, were 'block lens' types P700 for the home market, and usually F700 for export cars;

'tripod' bars were certainly fitted on earlier TR4s. Separate bulbs were still used, but progress arrived during the TR4 run when some later cars were fitted with sealed beam units. Rims, rubber seals and headlight fittings have already been described in the TR2/3/3A section.

TR4As all used sealed beam units, the Lucas type number F700 appearing to cover all applications despite the fact that these units clearly differ from earlier F700 types. This F700 designation, in fact, appears to cover all headlights fitted through to the end of the TR6. Although different lens patterns were used to cater for various export markets, Lucas did not see fit to number the different units individually, which makes things difficult for those aspiring to

exact originality. The dip switch remained the floor-mounted and foot-operated type 103SA until late 1972, when this archaic practice finally gave way on the CR/CF series TR6s to a hand-operated switch mounted on the left of the steering column.

Rear lamps are at first sight identical on the TR4/4A/5 models, being a combined reflector, brake light, tail light and direction indicator unit of Lucas type 669. A deep chromed bezel surrounds the whole, with a separate horizontal chromed bar dividing the orange flasher lens (on home market cars) at the top from the central reflector. In fact, the rear tail light lens on late TR4s, TR4As and TR5s has a vertical embossed pattern (type number 799), whereas earlier TR4s had a lens with a circular 'swirl' pat-

This is a very late TR4 wearing chromed wire wheels, which are probably not original. The exhaust system is also non-standard. Sun visors were an optional extra on TR4s and are fitted on this car.

tern. Reversing lights of type 661 were listed as optional on TR4s and TR4As, but the TR5 had standard reversing lights of type 594, with domed frosted glass lenses and a chromed bezel, mounted below the rear light units. Number plate illumination on TR4/4A/5 cars was provided by two chromed, domed Lucas 550 units, one let into each rear overrider, where they usefully also illuminated the luggage area with the boot opened. German market TR4/4A/5 models had the TR3A type of number plate light and special plain overriders.

TR4 sidelights comprised very small Lucas type 658 items with frosted plastic lenses, fitted outboard of the headlights and let into the top corners of the grille. Separate amber flasher lights, of the usual domed, glass lens, chromed bezel Lucas 594 type, were fitted to TR4/4A/5 models and again let into the grille, this time at each bottom corner. The flasher unit was type FL5 on the TR4/4A, 8FL on the TR5. The TR4A and TR5 had the type 658 front sidelights combined with a flasher repeater unit (type 771) and incorporated in a chromed moulding at the front of each wing, this moulding forming the front section of the side flash added to these cars. The TR5/250 had rear red marker lights (type 734) sited low down on

The late type of TR4 bonnet bulge, which extends right to the rear edge of the bonnet, continued for the TR4A.

the rear wings. Also on left-hand drive examples of these models, a hazard warning light system using the flashers appeared for the first time, but was not fitted on all cars.

The TR6's headlights continued as described for the previous models, but entirely new combined flasher and front side/marker light units (Lucas type 827) were fitted in the front valance above the bumper. Flashing indicator repeater lights (type 844) were fitted to the front wings forward of the wheel arches, although type 827, incorporating reflector units, were

fitted to US specification cars. Late US specification cars had entirely different front flashers/sidelights, these having to be let into the front bumper to allow room for the black 'safety' overriders.

At the rear, entirely new light units were fitted to the TR6. These were of 'strip' pattern, the outer lamp being the flasher which wrapped round the rear corners of the car.. At the inner end of each of these type 832 light units were reversing lights, while in the middle were the stop/tail lamp unit and a square reflex reflector. A chromed bezel

Showing on this TR5 is the original fitment driver's door mirror, standard on TR5s. A similar mirror could be purchased as an accessory for the passenger's side. Although the grille no longer allows for a starting handle, the lower valance is still indented! In case the vigilant reader is puzzled, this particular car was specially fitted for the photographic session with wire wheels on one side and Rostyle disc wheels on the other! The TR5 front valance had two cooling slots, seen below the number plate, and also a towing eye, not visible here.

This TR4A angle displays Michelotti's timeless lines to advantage. The boot rack is of a correct type for the period. The 'bullet' type 'speed' mirrors were a common accessory in the 1960s, and were in fact offered as an extra by Triumph. The wheels are the appropriate 60-spoke wires, fitted with knock-off nuts. This car's year, 1967, was the last in which knock-off nuts were fitted.

surrounded the whole light unit. Number plate illumination on the TR6 was originally by a chromed 'strip' light (type 766) mounted on top of the rear bumper, but the CR/CF series cars had a different light (believed to be type 908) moved to the underside of the number plate recess.

The TR6 finally saw an interior light added to the specification, by having a tunnel-mounted light and switch combined, together with a glovebox light. This continued until the introduction of the CR/CF series saw twin interior lights, one shining into each footwell, operated by a switch mounted on the gear lever console and courtesy switches on each 'A' post. TR6s also possessed a small boot light positioned in the front 'wall' of the boot interior under a translucent plastic cover, operated by raising the boot lid.

BODIES & BODY TRIM

As with the 'sidescreen' car bodies, much use was made of bolt-on outer panels, although the inner body structure, of course, was welded. No aluminium panelling was used (except for the early Surrey hardtop centre section), pressed steel of 19

A rear view of a TR250 roadster, sporting a period boot rack. The neat hoodstick cover is seen fitted. Some TR250s, it is believed, had the larger 'Monza' type fuel filler cap as standard equipment.

or 20swg being employed in the main. The bodies were manufactured 'in house' at the new plant at Speke in Liverpool and delivered as complete shells to Triumph's Coventry works for final assembly. The basic structure and method of construction was broadly similar to that used for the earlier TRs, and has been described in the previous chapter – but the body, of course, was much more modern.

Although at first glance the TR6 body seems very different from the TR4/4A/5 type, in reality it was a clever facelift performed in double-quick time by the German firm of Karmann. The central and inner sections remained almost the same, the facelift being effected by new wings, bonnet, boot, front/rear panels and valences. For this reason, I am treating all the 'winding window' TRs as the same from the body point of view.

A front-hinged bonnet with internal hinges was used for the first time on the TR4, immeasurably improving access to the radiator area and greatly facilitating engine removal. An internal release mechanism was used, with the catchplate assembly mounted on the bulkhead on the carburettor side of the engine. The bonnet of the TR4 needed a 'power-bulge' to clear the carburettor tops and allow for engine movement; although this necessity disappeared with the fuel-injected TR5, the bulge remained as a nice irrelevance until the TR6 restyle. In fact, there are four different TR4/4A/5 bonnets: the first type fitted up to CT 6429 has a short power bulge; the second type fitted from CT 6429 to body number CT 37689 differs in having the power bulge extended almost to the rear edge of the bonnet, and in losing the sockets for the bonnet location pegs on the trailing corners; the third type, fitted to TR4s from body number CT37690 and all TR4As, was basically the same but with detail differences; and the TR5 type retains the long bulge but has altered holes for the different badging. The TR6 bonnet was unique to the model and there is only one type. All bonnets were manually propped by a black painted 'bent-wire' prop mounted on the bonnet and engaging in a holder on the offside front wheel arch top.

Wings on the TR4/4A/5 did not vary, with the exception of drillings for differing external trim and lighting arrangements; again, TR6 wings are unique to the model. Doors are also broadly similar, this time throughout the range; a TR6 door can be made to fit a TR4 and *vice versa*. Doors,

however, differ in detail regarding locks, handles and internal and external trim. The winding windows fitted to all these cars were of a frameless design that can cause sealing and alignment problems. Door glasses remained the same throughout, but the raising and lowering mechanism was changed. The earlier 'scissors' type found on the TR4 and TR4A was not wholly satisfactory in use, so there was a different design for the later cars. The two-piece 'A' post and the 'B' post were also similar, differing throughout the range only in detail; the latch plate on TR5 and TR6 'B' posts differed from the earlier type in being of the anti-burst design. An inner and outer sill assembly, with a filler piece at each end, was fitted, the sill being welded to brackets which bolted to the floor and chassis. Floors were ribbed pressings, and minor changes were made to these, and to the transmission tunnel, from the TR4A onwards because of the altered handbrake position. Surprisingly, the holes in the floors used for the TR4 type jack remained to puzzle owners of later TRs! The rear bulkhead was built up from a deck assembly spanning the area behind the cockpit, a tonneau panel on each side, and the rear inner wings (to which separate wheel arch panels were welded).

Slight negative camber can be detected on the rear wheels of the TR6 even when stationary – the tail-squat is known well to those who drive in and behind IRS TRs. Dark paintwork suits the TR6 particularly well.

Unlike the later cars, the TR4/4A door handle had the key hole integral with the handle rather than separate and below it.

Between the wheelarches was a pressed occasional rear seat pan and a vertical heel board connecting to the rear of the transmission tunnel. The forward end of the transmission was covered by a bolted-in gearbox cover, similar to that of the TR3A but now made in pressure-moulded fibreboard to improve sound deadening. Since some rigidity was lost by this piece no longer being in steel, a 'Y' shaped console bracket connected the dashboard to the floors and chassis, straddling the gearbox cover.

At the rear, the spare wheel still sat in a sheet steel pan, but access was now through the boot rather than from a separate trapdoor. To the boot floor pan were welded stepped side floors with welded brackets to bolt to the chassis. The rear of the car was completed by a new valance, which was welded at the top on both sides to the side tonneau panels, the boot aperture thus being formed. Steel housings for the rear light units were welded to the inner wings and the bolted-up outer rear wings closed over them. The boot lid, with chromed external hinges and a bolted-on internal framework for strength, had a self-propping stay that was usually left unpainted. Very early TR4s had a manual prop, rather

like the one used for the bonnet.

At the front of the body was a two-piece valance: the upper part had holes for the headlights and the lower part had a starting handle cut-out (the handle also passing through a hole in the upper valance). The TR4A's upper valance differed in detail, but the lower valance was like the TR4's, the starting handle aperture remaining although the handle itself was no longer specified. The TR5 lower valance gained a central cut-out, presumably for cooling, while the starting handle cut-out continued even though the new grille no longer catered for this. As at the back, inner wings were welded to the wheel arches and at their rear ends to a large central bulkhead pressing, which had end panel assemblies closing each side. A separate scuttle assembly in two pieces was welded across the top of the back of the bulkhead to complete the front end of the body.

Despite its different appearance, the TR6 body was built up in much the same way. The near-flat boot lid now had internal hinges and an integral stiffening framework; also a fixed rear panel was incorporated. The front valance was now a one-piece unit with two cooling slots, and the CR/CF series TR6s had a separate black

moulded spoiler in addition.

The inner body panelwork, floors and areas under the bonnet and the wheel arches should be painted in external body colour on all these cars.

Door sealing was achieved by a rubber outer seal and an inner draught excluder described in the parts list as 'Snappon' – this appears to have been a development of the old 'Furflex' type of seal. On cars built with 'Surrey' hardtops, the sealing continued unbroken from the rear of the door aperture up the hardtop frame itself to the top of the door window glass. The Furflex continued

This rear view of an early CP series TR6 shows the number plate light mounted on the rear bumper and the joins in the three-piece bumper. The fuel filler is the early type, as used on previous TR models.

The CR/CF TR6s had no number plate light on the bumper – twin lights were fitted in the recess above the plate on the rear valance. The rear badgework can just be seen, the word 'injection' appearing in addition to the model designation on fuel-injected cars.

A 1975/6 specification North American CF TR6, showing part of the black front spoiler and the different front sidelights and flashers fitted because of the large 'safety' *overriders. Also visible on the wheel is one of the polished rim finishers fitted to many North American specification TR6s (Bill Piggott photo).*

over the top of the leading edge of the hardtop rear window. The trailing edge of the bonnet had a rubber seal inserted along the scuttle top and the boot had a rubber seal all round the aperture. A rubber seal and a separate weatherstrip were fitted in the tops of the doors.

Concerning external body fittings, these cars were manufactured in what was still the 'chrome' age, but the beginnings of the 'matt black' age caught up with later TR6s. TR4s and TR4As have chromed exterior door handles incorporating key locking on the driver's and passenger's sides. Inside, TR4/4A door fittings are chromed: there are cranked window winder handles with black plastic knobs, a door pull handle at the top of the door trim, and a door release and locking handle at the front of the door. The TR5 and early TR6 had no separate pull handle, a moulding in the door top rail trim sufficing; CR and CF series TR6s had a door pull 'pocket' incorporated in the centre of the door internal panel. These cars also

incorporated modern style 'safer' internal handles and window winders. The chromed external handles on the TR5 and TR6 were slimmer, while a separate lock was now fitted on each side a couple of inches below the handles.

The boot handle, a chromed 'T' handle below the number plate with a lock incorporated, was the same on TR4/4A/5 models. Boot locking on the TR6 was achieved by a chromed twist-type lock mounted on the fixed rear panel, causing the lid to spring up from the catch sufficiently to raise it. A self-propping stay for the bootlid was fitted on the nearside.

Chromed bumpers (with black brackets) were fitted to all these cars. The TR4 had a heavy duty front bumper, with twin overriders, mounted on substantial brackets bolted to the forward end of the chassis, with extra bracing pieces connecting the overriders to the front wheel arches, and brackets stiffening the bumper internally. The TR4A front bumper's overriders were

moved much nearer to the outer ends of the bumper blade, outboard of the headlamps. This necessitated redrilling the original blade, the overriders themselves were shorter, and the stays to the wheel arches were deleted. The TR4A front bumper continued for the TR5, but the TR6 was given new 'slimline' bumpers. There are four types of the TR6 front bumper: first is the CP/CC 'no spoiler' type; second is the CR/CF type with a spoiler; third is the 1974 US type with rubber overriders; and last is the 1975 US type with rubber overriders and repositioned sidelights and flashers. Cars from CR1 and CF1 were given extra, more substantial, fixings for their front bumpers, presumably inspired by North American parking habits!

The rear bumper was the same on TR4/4A/5 models – again a substantial chromed blade with twin overriders, these incorporating the number plate illumination. The rear bumper wrapped around the bodywork corners, and consequently was

This view shows the TR4's polished aluminium grille, with starting handle hole and small front marker/sidelights. The headlamps are modern halogen units and the interior mirror, which can just be seen, is not of the correct type. Note how one wiper arm is cranked to clear the scuttle ventilator when this is opened. The 'Triumph' lettering was carried over from the TR3A.

The TR4A grille still contained a starting handle hole, even though no dog was fitted on the crankshaft and there was no hole in the radiator! The different bumper and overrider spacing and can clearly be seen. There are two TR4A grille styles: the later type, shown here, has more squared-off edges to the bars. The headlamp is the correct Lucas item. The screen trim finisher is missing on this car.

This 'CP' TR6 has a stainless steel finishing strip along the base of the grille, but this should be black plastic on a 1970 car. The front flashing indicator repeaters are present on all cars, and the towing eye can just be seen.

bracketed not only to the chassis at the overrider mounting area, but also to the ends of the rear chassis cross tube by outriggers attaching to the bumper sides. In addition, further small brackets tied the base of the rear overriders directly to the chassis. Again, the TR6 has a unique rear bumper, a three-piece item formed of a central blade with two corner sections to give side protection. A black joint washer and joint plate is used each side to connect the three pieces. The central blade attaches to the chassis by the usual two substantial brackets, and outriggers to the rear chassis cross tube support the forward ends of the outer sections. There are three types of TR6 rear bumper central section: one accommodates the earlier number plate light on top of the bumper; a second plain type was used on CR/CF series cars; and a third US type appeared to take account of the large rubber overriders fitted on 1974–76 cars. This last type also necessitated modified side sections as these were now fixed higher on the body.

All four models use differing radiator grilles. The TR4 grille, bearing a family resemblance to the cellular TR3A type, was manufactured from similar pressed polished aluminium sheet. It was stayed to the front valance and incorporated cut-outs for the headlamps, starting handle, sidelamps, flasher units and overrider supports. The TR4A type is composed just of horizontal bars, with the exception of a single central inset vertical bar. Like the TR4 type, it is a one-piece grille and the leading edges of the horizontal bars are polished. The TR5 grille is very similar, but has matt black paint on the parts of the horizontal bars that face upwards, the sharper leading edges of the bars still being polished. The bottom horizontal bar was no longer scalloped to clear the non-existent starting handle, unlike on the TR4A.

The TR6 had a matt black 'chip-cutter' grille, inset slightly and having at its centre an almost rectangular 'TR6' badge. A horizontal channel-section bar divided the

The head-on view of the CR series TR6 shows the later grille with chrome trim top and bottom. The front bumper had more substantial fittings on these cars and was slightly further forward, which made room for the front spoiler. The 'TR6' badge was finished in vitreous enamel. On these later TR6s, matt black wiper blades and arms are correct.

Detail of the TR4's rear badging and boot handle. To the extreme right can just be seen one of the number plate lights, let into the side of the overrider.

This bonnet badge was used only on the TR4A.

Two types of 'IRS' badge were used on the TR4A's boot lid. This one has a thick bar linking the letters – the other has a significantly thinner bar.

The TR4 bonnet medallion – this style of badge was not used on subsequent models. The word 'Triumph' does not appear as it was mounted on the bonnet in separate letters.

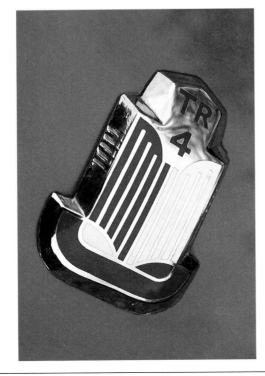

The TR5 announced its engine capacity on its flanks; the red side marker lights were fitted even on UK and European specification cars, although only required in North America. The red lens correctly has a screw at one end and a clip at the other.

TR250 boot lid badgework; the 'TR250' badge appeared also on the rear wings (Bill Piggott photo).

Petrol injection was big news on a production car in 1967, so the TR5's boot lid badge boasted the fact. The ground colour of the badge was pale beige, with a black background for the 'PI' section.

middle of the grille, matt black tape within the channel making it appear as if twin narrowly-spaced bars were in fact fitted. There were two TR6 grilles; CR/CF series cars had a stainless steel beading fitted to the top and bottom of the grille, which in my view somewhat spoils the effect.

Badges on the TR4 again were largely carried over from the TR3A. The familiar blue and white front medallion, bearing the legend 'TR4', was fitted in the centre of the bonnet about 6in back from the leading edge. In front of this were individual letters forming the word 'TRIUMPH', as on the later TR3As. These same letters were used on the boot lid, fitted into pre-drilled holes at the point where the boot lid turned downwards. The only other badge was a new chrome-on-Mazak 'TR4' in script, fitted towards the bottom right corner of the boot lid.

TR4As continued to use the Triumph lettering front and rear, but the medallion was finally consigned to history and replaced by a round plastic badge with a chromed Mazak surround depicting an updated version of the old Triumph 'globe' motif. At the rear, the script badge had the letter 'A' added, and – so that the neighbours could be in no doubt – 'IRS' was also added (but not on North American solid axle TR4As of course).

The TR5 brought further badgework updating, the 'TRIUMPH' lettering now disappearing. At the front, the only badge was a beige/cream enamelled motif, with an inverted trapezium shape, carrying 'TR5' in chrome and having a chromed edge. Somewhat eccentrically, this badge was fitted off the centre line of the bonnet, to the right as viewed from the front – but this did add character to the car! At the side,

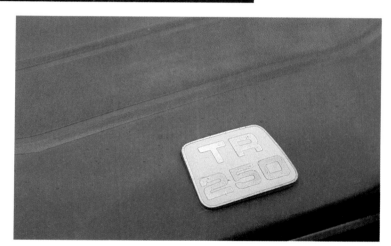

The 'TR250' bonnet badge was in the same colours as the 'TR5' one, but the trapezium shape was inverted for the TR5.

Unique to the TR5/250 was a narrow chromed strip below the door on the outer sill. The Rostyle wheels are visible here, as are the standard equipment sun visors with a vanity mirror on the passenger's side. The key hole is now separate from the door handle.

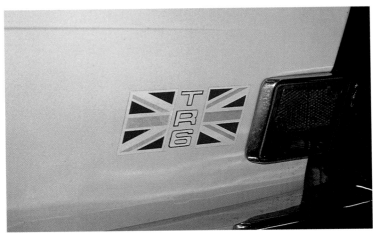

North American specification CF TR6s had this 'Union Flag' decal on the rear wings. This one is an original transfer but it has faded with the passage of time (Bill Piggott photo).

The correct standard door mirror mounted on the driver's side door of a TR5. It was a universal type and could be assembled 'other-handed' for use on the passenger's door.

on the rear wings just above the marker lights, were chromed rectangular badges stating '2500' in black lettering. At the rear on the right-hand side of the boot lid, the TR5 carried the maker's name in chromed lettering on a beige/cream rectangular surround with a chromed edge. When overdrive was fitted, a further badge announcing this fact was added, and below this was yet another badge, a beige/cream and chromed item reading 'TR5 PI'. The 'PI' letters, standing for petrol injection, were in cream on a dark background, presumably to emphasise this feature – big news in 1967.

The TR250 also had unique badging. The bonnet badge, the same shape and colour as the TR5's, read 'TR250'. The rear bore the same 'Triumph' badge, and below it the designation 'TR250' on a badge equi-

valent to the 'TR5PI' one, only this was entirely cream/beige with chromed lettering, with no dark shading. Also unique to the TR250 were its US-style triple nose stripes in a reflective light silver paint; a central thick band with a thin band each side of it ran across the bonnet laterally, and down each front wing to the wheelarch opening. It is uncertain whether these stripes were applied at the factory or in the USA by supplying dealers. A photograph exists showing a TR250 on the Coventry production line carrying this striping, but other evidence suggests that it was applied in the USA. Perhaps it was a combination of the two!

As for the TR6's badging, the central grille motif has already been described. The maker's name appeared only on a black

badge with chrome lettering on the rear panel, sited on the right-hand side between the boot lid top and the rear light unit. Just below this was a second chromed badge bearing the word 'Injection' on non-North American TR6s. A chromed badge announcing 'overdrive' was also added if applicable. On each rear wing forward of the rear light were transfers stating 'TR6', the colour of these depending on body colour. White transfers were used on most cars, although yellow cars had black decals and white cars had red ones. CF series cars for North America had these transfers in the form of a Union Flag split down the middle with the letters 'TR6' placed vertically between the two halves of the flag. Finally, the British Leyland corporate image caught up with the TR series towards the end of

The windscreen surround is correct in black on this 1970 TR6, but 1969 models had the screen surround in body colour. A lift-up heater vent is fitted and the satin finish wiper arms are correct.

The windscreen top capping rail from a 'Surrey' hard top equipped car. The centre section bolts through the two large holes.

CR/CF series TR6s had this black plastic grille substituted for the earlier ventilation/heater intake flap. Although there was no longer any need for it, the wiper arm remained cranked. Note the position of the screen wash jets.

1971, when the Leyland 'plughole' motif appeared towards the bottom of each front wing.

The TR4 carried no other external chromed decoration save that already referred to in this and earlier sections, although one must not overlook the stainless steel wing beading that ran along the edge of all the outer wings, including down the rear of the car under the light units. This beading was used also on TR4As. On TR5s alone, all this beading was oversprayed body colour for some reason. The TR6 carried wing beading only on the rear wing top, and then only up to CP/CC 50000. A polished aluminium capping rail finished off the top of the rear of the TR4 cockpit, the hood fixings being accommodated in this. The TR4A had a stainless steel finish-

ing strip running from a point on the door just above the handle to meet the chromed side light and indicator repeater unit on the front wing. This same type of strip was present also on the TR5, although it was slightly wider. The TR5 also had a narrow stainless steel trim strip running between the front and rear wheel arches, on the outer edge of the sill just below the door. TR6s shared this sill trim, but did not have the door to front wing strip.

The TR5 was the first TR to be given an external mirror as standard, a single chrome finished mirror being mounted on the driver's door. A matching one for the passenger's side could be added as an accessory. The TR6 reverted to the earlier practice of not having an external mirror as standard, but owners frequently fitted them.

Matching shots of Derek Pollock's TR4 with and without the 'solid' roof centre section, which was secured by four bolts. Early on this section was made of aluminium, but most cars have less vulnerable steel items. Many owners over the years have arrived home after a pleasant evening drive with the centre section removed, laid it in place temporarily to weatherproof the car overnight, and driven off next morning forgetting to fix the bolts . . .

A Surrey top in position. Although the term 'Surrey top' is now used generically to mean the entire hard top unit, originally it referred just to the soft centre section seen here. This fitted over a lightweight framework and was held by press-studs. The side flaps to the Surrey section look somewhat deep on this car. The bullet-type wing mirror is of the period, and the positioning of the radio aerial by the rear window was recommended. Note the panoramic rear vision offered through the hardtop rear section.

The TR5 type mirror was available to special order on TR6s up to 1973. Following that date, a more modern door mirror was offered.

The internal mirror was no longer scuttle-mounted, but suspended from the screen top rail. The TR4 type had a black stalk and a matt black back and edging. This same type was fitted to some TR4As but an alternative type with square corners was also used – but the parts catalogue gives no clue as to which was used when. The TR5 had a dipping mirror that was collapsible in the event of impact; it was no longer rectangular, being shorter along the top edge than the bottom and having rounded corners, particularly at the top. This same black finished mirror was used on most of the TR6s, although hardtop models were listed as having a different type which appears to have been wider to offer a greater field of view.

Windscreens were basically similar throughout the series. The pressed steel frame had at each bottom corner a peg which engaged in a hidden socket and bracket arrangement mounted within the scuttle top area, the peg having a securing nut at its base. All these cars, therefore, had removable windscreens, although rust and lack of use of the facility over the years can make you doubt the fact. The same complete windscreen assembly part number is listed for TR4As through to TR6s, but the TR4 assembly has different hood top rail fixings. TR4s and TR4As had only a rubber seal at the screen frame base, but the later cars had an additional internal black plastic finishing strip at this point. They also had matt black side finishers at either side of the screen, and along the top horizontal internal part of the windscreen assembly. The screen glass itself was retained by a rubber seal with an inserted chrome or satin finish moulding. Glasses were toughened as standard, but laminated glass was an optional extra which was usually fitted on TR6s. Screen frames on TR4/4A/5 models were finished in body colour, but TR6 frames were matt black – with the exception of 1969 model year cars (up to CP 50001) which also had body colour frames.

The spare wheel was accommodated in a well formed at the base of the boot on TR4/4A/5 models. An upwards-facing hook was bolted through the boot floor pan to the chassis cross-tube roughly in its centre, and this engaged with a loose hook, washer and wing nut which passed through the wheel centre to clamp the spare wheel

These are the correct seats for a late TR4, although this car carries a non-original centre console between them.

down. A wheel-changing tool strap was also fitted in the boot. The wheel itself was covered by a hardboard panel forming a floor for luggage, this having a short strap and press stud arrangement at either side at the rear to secure it. On the TR5, this board was stepped up slightly because of the wider wheel, marginally reducing boot space. The TR6's spare wheel was in the same relative position with similar securing arrangements, but access was much more awkward as the boot no longer opened down to bumper level. Again a false boot floor was provided by a hardboard panel, attached by a single half-turn fastener.

Two very different types of hardtops existed. Introduced with the TR4 was the then-unique 'Surrey' top, later reinvented by several continental manufacturers as the 'Targa' top. This consisted of a cast aluminium rear frame incorporating a wrap-around rear window; it was semi-permanently bolted to the car and gave as an ancillary benefit some measure of roll-over protection. Between the rear window frame and the windscreen frame one normally had a steel roof section (although those on early TR4s were made in aluminium), this having two fixing bolts each at front and rear to fix it to the screen and rear frame, forming a secure hardtop. As the centre section was too big to be carried in the car when removed, a temporary centre cover of hooding material was available to fill the gap. This stretched over a lightweight folding framework that pegged and clipped into the windscreen top and the

rear screen surround. The whole arrangement was most ingenious and worked well, its only disadvantage being its expense. It could be ordered new with the car, or fitted as an after-market conversion. Cars built with Surrey tops were not normally supplied with hoods or hoodsticks. Surrey tops were also available for TR4As and TR5s. When supplied with a new car, they were normally finished in body colour, although contrasting colours (usually black or white) could be ordered. The TR4A/5 top differed slightly from the TR4 one in the type of fixing bolts and spacers used. TR5 hardtops had fixing bolts in either chrome or 'blackadized' finished (a factory name for matt black).

The TR6 had a completely different one-piece hardtop more suited to the car's angular lines. Again, this could be ordered with the car or fitted later, and in matching (more usual) or contrasting (quite rare) colours. This all-steel hardtop was fully trimmed and had fixed rear quarter windows positioned for maximum all-round visibility. Since it was bolted firmly in place, it added considerably to the rigidity of the car (like the Surrey top), as well as rendering it potentially more weather- and thief-proof.

DIMENSIONS

TR4/4A

Length	12ft 11½in	3.96m
Width	4ft 9½in	1.46m
Height (hood up)	4ft 2in	1.27m
Wheelbase	7ft 4in	2.23m
Dry weight	2128lb	970kg
Kerb weight	2240lb	1015kg

TR5 (exceptions to above)

Dry weight	2152lb	981kg
Kerb weight	2268lb	1034kg

TR6 PI

Length	13ft 3in	4.04m
Width	4ft 10in	1.47m
Height (hood up)	4ft 2in	1.27m
Wheelbase	7ft 4in	2.23m
Dry weight	2290lb	1041kg
Kerb weight	2408lb	1085kg

TR6 carburettor (exceptions to above)

Length (1973/4 cars)	13ft 6in	4.12m
Length (1975/6 cars)	13ft 7½in	4.16m
Kerb weight	2470	1120kg

NB: Cars fitted with wire wheels were wider: TR4/4A/5 width became 5ft, TR6 width became 5ft 1in. TR4A models with IRS differed slightly from the dry and kerb weights given for the TR4. The TR250 was approximately 30lb lighter than the TR5. Kerb weights for the TR6 carburettor cars depended upon export specification, the figure given being the maximum weight which applied to the final cars.

Unless leather was specified, TR4A seats were trimmed in ICI 'Ambla', which superseded 'Vynide'. This colour is Midnight Blue. Incidentally, the piping was always in plastic, even where the seat trim was leather. The screw that can just be seen on the door pocket is correct, but the bright blue 'Furflex' around the door aperture is the wrong colour, and should be darker. Handbrake gaiters varied in their bagginess, this one possibly erring on the loose side!

The TR4 rear compartment showing the ledge on which the optional occasional seat would sit. Seat belt mountings are in the right position for the static type of belts, and the carpeting and pleated rear bulkhead panel are correct. In roadster versions of the TR4, this rear panel (with rather thicker padding) concealed the hood, lifting up with the side pieces to allow access.

The TR5 type seats were unique to the model, these being original and correct. The door top trim now incorporated the pull handle in its moulding. The small area of white paint showing at the rear of this trim piece is correct, but the inertia reel belts in this car are not original – the correct type was mounted on the vertical face of the wheel arch. The trim was now in 'embossed Ambla'. The later style 'B' post and catch plate assembly can be seen.

INTERIOR TRIM, BOOT & HOOD

Early TR4s had TR3A bucket seats up-holstered in Vynide or optional leather. Both seats were adjustable on floor-mounted sliding runners (painted grey or silver), and the driver's folded forwards to give access to the rear space. These seats continued until approximately the end of 1962, when, at body number 15076CT, a completely new design of TR4 seat was substituted. In this design, the whole seat tipped forward, whereas with the earlier seats only the backrest tipped. From body number CT20925 both seats were made to tip forward. The new seats had flatter, wider seat cushions, and squabs that were more right-angled in section at the top. The seat frames were entirely new, and the seats were now filled with foam rubber over a rubber stretcher plate, rather than the old 'springs and horsehair' system. All seats had piping, frequently in white but also quite commonly the same colour as the upholstery.

An occasional rear seat cushion was an optional extra, this being a rectangular seat, with piping and longitudinal pleating, fitting directly on the existing ledge. Whether or not the occasional seat was ordered, pleated lift-up panels were fitted at the rear and sides of the rear compartment

Seen here are the correct CP series seats as supplied on non-North American TR6s, with no provision for head rests. However, from the 1970 model year the seats reclined, the reclining mechanism operated by a chromed lever. The black plastic lever was provided to release the seat tipping mechanism. Both seats had release catches, even though no occasional rear seat was listed! The correct type of 'Furflex' trim around the door aperture is visible.

on the roadster (as opposed to Surrey top) models; these neatly hid the hood and hoodsticks. Cars supplied new with hardtops had fixed, non-padded panels at this point. The occasional rear seat continued to be listed for the TR4A, although its practicality was reduced because the TR4A's new folding hood occupied much of the rear space when lowered. The rear seat does not appear to have been available on the TR5.

Seats on the TR4A were similar in overall shape to the later TR4 type, but were now more heavily padded and upholstered in

ICI's then-new 'Ambla' material rather than Vynide. Leather continued as an option, as it did on the TR5, but it was specified with decreasing frequency. Whereas the later TR4 seat had longitudinal pleats over the whole cushion and squab area, the TR4A seat had pleating only in the cushion and squab centre sections, a padded, rolled edge being incorporated in addition. The piping on the top of the TR4A squabs also continued further towards the rear of the seat top, which had a less angular contour than the late TR4 type.

TR5 seats were again in Ambla and

These are the later CR series TR6 fire-resistant seats, on which headrests were an optional extra. These seats were all foam-padded, no springing nor stuffing being employed. TR6s did not have contrasting piping on the trim.

Even on TR6s equipped with the hard top from new, no occasional rear seat cushion was offered. Here the later type of rear bulkhead trim is shown. The carpeting is correct and original.

A correct TR4 door trim, showing the map pocket, interior handles, door lock and striker arrangements. The Vynide material could be either fine or coarse grained.

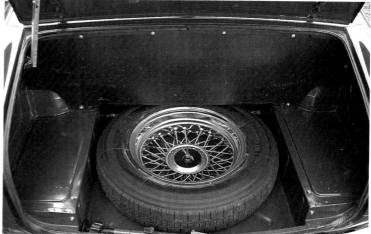

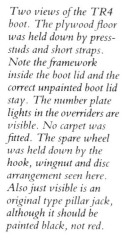

Two views of the TR4 boot. The plywood floor was held down by press-studs and short straps. Note the framework inside the boot lid and the correct unpainted boot lid stay. The number plate lights in the overriders are visible. No carpet was fitted. The spare wheel was held down by the hook, wingnut and disc arrangement seen here. Also just visible is an original type pillar jack, although it should be painted black, not red.

altered only in detail. The pleated sections now contained numerous 'breathing holes' and the pleats ran right to the front of the cushions. Road testers commented on their greater comfort and thigh support, but these seats were still non-reclining and no provision for fitting headrests was made. Catches were now incorporated in the tipping mechanism to ensure that the seats did not pivot under hard braking.

TR6s had a multiplicity of different types of seat. Early non-US cars had a development of the TR5 seat, but the pleating, still with breathing holes, now ran laterally. Padded rolls were fitted all round the central pleats. On these early types, there was still no reclining mechanism nor headrest provision. The early North American seat had a high back with a built-in headrest, the lateral pleating running right into this angled forward headrest. From CP/CC 50001 onwards, at the start of the 1970 model year, a reclining mechanism was at last added, a chromed operating lever being fitted on the outside of each seat, roughly at the point where the cushion meets the squab. The black-painted lever that operated the seat release catch was situated at almost the same point. The 'high-back' US seat continued with various modifications, some inspired by US safety legislation which caused frames and runners to be strengthened, until the CR and CF series cars arrived at the end of 1972. At this point, a single seat for all markets was introduced; it had provision for a separate adjustable head restraint, trimmed and padded to match. Pleating and trim rolls on the seat were broadly as before. It is thought that cars supplied to North America, and possibly other export markets, were always fitted with head restraints for legislative reasons, but

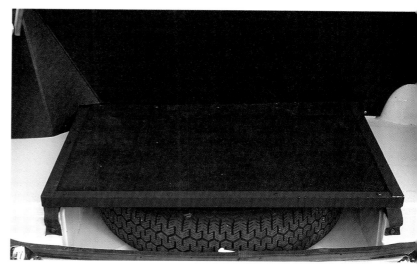

certainly they remained an option on UK-supplied cars – but more often than not they were fitted. Small blanking plugs were provided for the seat tops where no restraints were ordered. Also from the CR/CF introduction point, seat cover material had a coarser grain. I should add that TR6 seats alone take up almost 60 pages of the 1973 TR6 parts catalogue, taking into account the many export and other variations, so it is regrettably not possible to list all the minutiae of their development here!

The rear compartment back trim panel described earlier continued largely unchanged, with vertical pleating, right through to early TR6s, although it no longer served to hide the hood and hoodsticks after the adoption of the folding hood on the TR4A. On later CR/CF series cars, this rear panel was of a plainer design with just two horizontal pleats.

Internal trim and carpet sections in the

Interior of the TR5 boot, showing how the black-painted plywood floor was now 'stepped' to clear the wider wheels that were now fitted. No carpet was ever fitted originally, while a tool strap should be found in the wheel well in the right-hand corner to retain the wheel-changing tools. The cross-section of the rubber boot seal is also incorrect on this car.

TR6 boots were carpeted and an interior light was fitted, operating automatically when the lid is lifted. Black millboard was used to line the boot, except at the back. The correct tool kit as supplied with later TR6s is shown, although the jack and handle were more usually green or black.

This is the correct TR4 interior mirror and mounting. Also correct, although optional extras on the TR4, are the padded sun visors on their matt black mounting bar.

the periphery of the arches. The rear quarter panel sections and door trims were in millboard covered in Vynide with unequally-spaced horizontal pleats. Door trims, incorporating slim Vynide map pockets, did not reach to the top of the doors on TR4s, the door tops being painted body colour. Black rubber gaiters sealed the base of the handbrake and the gear lever. The boot interior had a black-painted millboard cover at its forward end over the petrol tank, but otherwise it was painted body colour and left untrimmed except for a black hardboard spare wheel cover.

The same basic trim layout was used on the TR4A and TR5, but with slight modifications. At the rear, the trim quarter panels and capping rail changed to suit the new hood design. As with the seats, Ambla replaced Vynide. The doors were now fully trimmed, a grained black plastic capping rail being added to the top of the door and overlapping the familiar trim panel. The handbrake was now on the transmission tunnel, and surrounded by an Ambla bag let into the carpet. Carpets replaced the footwell rubber mats, although on the driver's side a rubber heel mat was still supplied. The underfelt now specified for the floor carpets was very much a mixed blessing, for it soaked up water and promoted floor corrosion. On the TR5, the door capping rail now incorporated a moulding to serve as a pull handle, the chromed handle being deleted.

Sun visors were listed as an option on the TR4, but from the TR4A they were

TR4 – and subsequent models except where later qualified – were as follows. The footwells had rubber mats with pleated heel sections; these were long enough to cover the lower inner front bulkhead and were held in place by press stud fasteners fixed to the floors. Carpet covered the rear floors, differential cover, transmission tunnel, gearbox cover, front bulkhead sides and rear around the gearbox tunnel join, inner wing area in the footwells, 'B' post reinforcement pads, heelboard and rear seat ledge, and sill edges. The carpet was edge-bound and either studded or glued into place as appropriate. The rear wheel arches were covered in slightly padded Vynide (in either coarse or fine grain) and piped around provided as standard. Made of white, padded, grained PVC, they were mounted on a three-piece cranked rail fixed at the centre and at both outer ends to the top of the windscreen frame. TR5 visors were slightly different and the passenger's incorporated a vanity mirror. The fitting arrangements were also altered and became rather more substantial. Sun visors on TR6s were similar but in black rather than white.

The TR6's interior trim was much the same as on the earlier cars, with the following differences. Leather as an option appears to have been deleted, although I have heard claims that some cars were delivered with leather trim from new and it is referred to in one edition of the parts manual. In the interests of sound deadening, underfelt was now fitted to the transmission tunnel and heelboard/lower rear bulkhead area. 'Fibroceta' insulating padding was fitted under the wheel arch trims, and further trim panels were placed above the gearbox tunnel under the dashboard area. The boot was now fully lined; a bound-edged carpet covered the floor and black casing board was fitted on all four sides. A turn buckle arrangement was now used to hold down the false floor above the spare wheel. The rubber gear lever surround was replaced by a PVC/ Ambla conical gaiter, described in the parts book as a 'gauntlet'! Door trims were still pleated and fitted with map pockets, but the number of pleats was reduced on CR/CF series cars. The rear bulkhead trim panel was modified as described earlier.

Safety belt mountings were incorporated from the start of the TR4 series in 1961. Static lap or diagonal belts were offered as an option on the TR4 and TR4A, but by the end of TR4A production, belts were legally required in several markets, including the UK. Belts, therefore, were normally fitted to new cars, but priced and quoted as an extra. It was as late as May 1972 when seat belts – static lap and diagonal belts – were finally fitted as standard and included in the list price; inertia reel belts still cost extra. The three-point static belts usually had their mountings on the rear wheelarch, at the base of the quarter panel, and on the side of the transmission tunnel rear.

The TR4 used a development of the somewhat outdated 'kit of parts' hood found on the TR3A – and on most other 1950s sports cars. Hoodsticks, consisting of three transverse bows linked by two bands of webbing, were permanently attached to the interior of the car on each side just behind the top of the door aperture. The

This view of a CR TR6's door interior shows the later type of door trim and anti-burst door latches. The stainless steel tread plate, however, is not original.

A side view of a TR4 roadster hood, showing the press-stud on the front corner (Bill Piggott photo).

The rear view of the same hood, showing the 'lift-a-dot' fasteners – 16 in total – which attached the hood to the polished alloy cockpit capping rail (Bill Piggott photo).

A rear quarter detail of the convertible hood fitted from the TR4A onwards, this one being on a TR250. 'Lift-a-dot' fasteners have given way to black press studs, fewer in number than the 'lift-a-dots' on the TR4 roadster (Bill Piggott photo).

The TR6's neat hood cover, which was standard equipment, is seen in position. However, the design of the convertible hood meant that it took up too much space when folded for an occasional rear seat still to be a realistic possibility. The early type interior light, seen on the transmission tunnel, should have a chromed surround. The press studs holding the cover and hood were known officially as 'plastic durable dots'.

hood itself, made from vinyl–coated canvas material in black or white with three 'Vybak' windows, was separate from the hoodsticks, although provision was made for storage of both items behind lift-up rear and side panels. The hood was attached at the rear by a series of 'lift-a-dot' fasteners on the rear tonneau capping rail. Elasticated straps along each side of the hood internally helped to keep the material taut above each side window, and the front edge of the hood was attached by a three-piece, full width, steel-reinforced tongue fitting beneath a lip on the top of the windscreen top rail, making a watertight seal. The outer front edges of the hood were fastened to the screen top by a press stud and hook arrangement. Side flaps projected downwards from the hood about 1½in, further to improve the weather sealing at the top of the side window glasses.

Although it took some time and trouble to erect, this hood had the advantage that it left the occasional rear seat area available for use, even when the hood was folded. This was not the case with the hood fitted from the TR4A onwards. This later hood, permanently fixed to the frame, was much quicker and more convenient to operate. This same basic design was used on all post–TR4 cars, with progressive development.

The new hood was too large when folded to stow behind the rear panel, so a separate hoodstick cover was provided, picking up on the rear tonneau fasteners. This 'convertible' hood had a black–painted steel

TR4 dashboard, painted white as normal and with the centre section in the correct black 'crackle' finish. Note the 'airflow' ventilators at each end of the dash and the integral grab handle below the glove box lid. The steering wheel is non-original but period (and the hornpush is correct). Extra switches have been fitted to the right of the steering wheel and a period map light has been added to the top of the dashboard.

transverse angle piece to attach it to the rear deck of the car, and at the front a header-rail was attached to the front of the hood. Below this was a channel which retained a rubber seal, this clamping down onto the top of the screen frame to provide a watertight seal. Two over-centre toggle catches provided the clamping mechanism. Unlike the previous hood, this new type had a positive link by scissors-action metal stays between the front and rear, these running along the top of the glass side windows. Their presence helped both sealing and tension, although the whole arrangement was more complicated and costly. The transverse hood bows were attached to these side supports, although two webbing straps were still used as well. Straps with press studs were provided at each front corner as an additional securing device. A row of external press studs was fitted at the rear of the hood to enable the hoodstick cover to be secured when the hood was lowered. These were polished on TR4A/5s, and black on TR6s.

The TR5 had a hood which, although similar to the TR4A type, was further refined and improved. The header rail differed, and the catches were now lever types that were turned through 90 degrees to wind the hood front hard down onto the screen frame. These catches were safer, as the levers were arranged so as not to project into the passenger space. Sealing was further improved by the side cant rails having two-piece rubber sections attached

to them, these rubbers being designed to seal to the side window glasses. In addition, velcro was used to ensure that the hood material sealed positively down onto the cant rails. The front corner press studs were deleted. Contemporary road testers praised this hood as one of the best of its type available, so it is not surprising that the hood used for the TR6 was basically identical, with the exception of the addition of a zip-out rear window. The parts manual refers to a special TR6 hood 'for German Markets only', but I have not been able to establish why this was done. TR250 and TR6 hoods for US cars frequently, but not invariably, had strips of silvery reflecting 'Scotchbrite' tape attached over and to the rear of the side windows, and also around the base of the hood at the rear.

As well as the hood cover supplied with the car, a full tonneau cover was always available as an extra (but standard on TR6s after December 1973) except on cars supplied with hardtops ex-factory. Press stud fixings were employed, and on the TR4 special chromed fittings were attached to the dashboard just behind the windscreen, both centrally and towards the edges in front of the air vents. Three press studs were also fitted along the tops of each door on TR4As onwards, although these appear to have been omitted on cars sold new with Surrey tops. The tonneau, which had the usual zip set slightly off-centre towards the passenger's side, was fixed at the rear by a row of press studs around the

rear cockpit finishing rail – but on TR4s it picked up on the 'lift-a-dot' fasterners. Tonneaux were made of the same plasticised canvas material used for hoods. In addition to the usual pocket for the steering wheel, pockets to accommodate headrests on later cars were included where appropriate.

DASHBOARD & INSTRUMENTS

The TR4 dashboard was a somewhat austere metal pressing, painted white irrespective of body colour. Spa White was used at first but replaced by New White in March 1963. At its outer ends it had the then-unique, but now universal, black 'airflow' ventilation grilles, later claimed to be 'reinvented' by Ford! A knurled wheel in each grille controlled and directed airflow. The lockable glovebox had a metal lid in white fitted with a chromed finger-grip escutcheon surrounding the lock. The central section of the dashboard was a trapezium-shaped panel with a black crackle finish, into which were let the minor instruments and pull-out ashtray.

In front of the driver on the left was the 5in speedometer with trip and on the right a matching 6000rpm rev counter. Most instruments were carried over onto the earlier TR4s from the TR3A, and have been described previously – but the temperature gauge became electrically rather than capilliary operated. Later TR4s and all TR4As still used the familiar TR instruments, but

The correct TR5 steering wheel is shown, although the leather rim has faded. The walnut veneer dashboard now has a matt finish. The gear lever gaiter is incorrect, but black bezels for the instruments are correct. Notice that the speedometer and rev counter positions were reversed on the TR5 compared with earlier cars. Note the 'eyeball' vent and 'safety' type rocker switches.

The superb interior of Ken Westwood's car, showing the TR4A's walnut veneer dashboard and the correct steering wheel and gearknob – but the gear lever rubber gaiter should be round rather than square. The carpeting is correct, but whether a rubber heel mat was originally fitted on the passenger's side, as shown here, is debateable. Note that the TR4A, unlike the TR4, has trimmed door tops.

The glove box on the TR5 had an interior light operated by a trip switch. There was no longer a finger pull on the glove box lock and the dashboard crash pad no longer incorporated a grab handle.

now the glasses were flat rather than convex. Also the four minor instruments were no longer fully open-faced, the tops of their needles now being shrouded. Between the speedometer and rev counter were set two warning lights (type WL11), green for indicators and red for ignition. Main beam warning was still indicated by an inset red lamp at the bottom of the speedometer. All instruments were internally illuminated.

The dashboard top, a black-grained plastic moulding with windscreen air vents, was slightly cowled over both the glovebox lid and the main instruments. A semi-padded black-grain moulded rail ran along the bottom of the dashboard, bowing out under the glovebox lid to form a grab handle. In the centre of this rail was a flat switch panel containing the ignition key lock, plus black and silver plastic knobs for the two-stage pull-out light switch, screen-wash button, wiper switch and choke control. Ignition keys were usually from the 'FP' or 'FS' series. Heater controls, where fitted, consisted of a temperature control which worked the hot water valve on the engine, a single-speed heater blower switch, and a distribution control. These were mounted on the bracing plate that anchored the dashboard to the floor via the transmission tunnel. Above the heater controls was a cut-out, blanked if necessary, for fitting a standard car radio. Panel light illumination was rheostatically controlled by a rotary switch situated on the dashboard outboard of the steering

column. The scuttle ventilator was operated by a cranked lever situated more or less centrally under the dashboard.

TR4 direction indicators were now worked by a steering column stalk, while the optional overdrive was operated by a stalk on the opposite side. These chromed stalks had black plastic fingergrips at their ends. A moulded black plastic handbrake grip was fitted. Pendant pedals were used, with rubber pads bearing a moulded 'T' for Triumph on the brake and clutch.

The TR4A layout was broadly similar, but the one-piece dashboard was now in polished walnut veneer to give a considerable uplift in quality – so much so that many TR4s have had a wooden dashboard retrofitted. In fact, certain late North American specification TR4s are believed to have had

A separate ignition key lock was still fitted to the TR5, the steering lock not becoming standard until 1971. The rotary switch between the two lower instruments is a panel light rheostat. The chromed bolt heads seen at the bottom should have black caps fitted, and black rather than bright screws should be used in the dashboard.

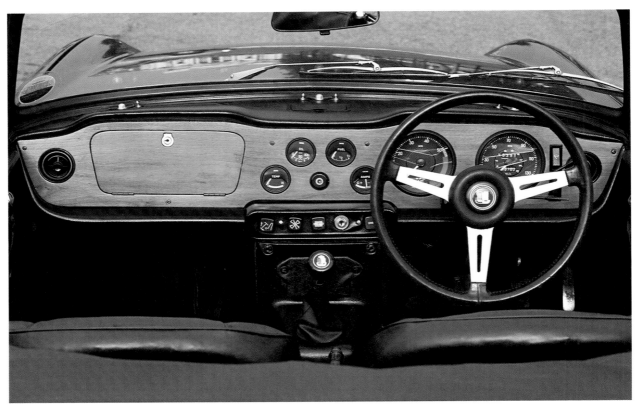

The CP series TR6 dashboard was very similar to the TR5 type. An ammeter was still fitted, together with an ignition key lock rather than a steering lock (up to 1971). The steering wheel and horn push shown here are correct, but the gear knob is wrong and the centre console where the radio fits has been modified. The bolts at the base of the screen should be black, not bright.

The TR6's ashtray was fitted into the top of the dashboard.

the walnut dashboard fitted from new. The rev counter had a red shaded area between 5000–6000rpm, instead of just a red line at 5000rpm; this type of rev counter was possibly also fitted to some later TR4s. The rheostat switch moved to the central switch panel, taking the place vacated by the light switch, which was now a three-position stalk mounted on the steering column and incorporating a headlamp flasher. Indicator and overdrive stalks were on the other side of the column. On the TR4A, the central console/bracing structure extended backwards to surround the gear lever base and

was somewhat padded, a different type of rubber gaiter being required for the base of the lever – which was slightly shortened – as a result. The bonnet release on both models was a white plastic knob situated below the right-hand side of the dashboard, even on left-hand drive cars.

The TR5 and TR250 retained a wooden dashboard, but in the interests of safety this was now in a non-reflective finish. The general layout was broadly similar to that of the TR4A. The moulded grab handle disappeared, while the ashtray moved to the top of the scuttle, being replaced in the centre of the dashboard by a new design of panel light rheostat switch in black with a white motif. The ventilation grilles were deleted in favour of modern swivelling eyeballs in black plastic. The switch gear was modernised, becoming recessed in the interests of safety. The same six instruments were fitted, but of a newer design with matt black bezels, matt black dials and white figures. The rev counter was now shaded yellow from 5000–5500rpm, and red above 5500rpm. The wipers and electric screenwashers were controlled by two elongated black 'safety' type rocker switches (made by Clear Hooters Ltd), and the heater fan was now two-speed and controlled from the recessed switch panel. Also

on this panel were knobs – now square-headed in black plastic with white motifs – for air distribution, heater temperature and cold start device, and also the ignition key. Within the 120mph speedometer were two warning lights for main beam and indicators, while the rev counter contained two more for charging and low oil pressure, this latter despite the continued presence of a pressure gauge. Other details continued much as described for the TR4A, with minor modifications.

The dashboard, instrument and control layout for the early TR6 was similar to the TR5/250, with the exception of the steering wheel described in the 'Steering' section. Even an ignition key/starter was still used rather than a steering column lock, although this modern feature finally arrived on the home market in early 1971 at CP 52786. Export specification cars had had a steering column lock somewhat earlier, possibly from CP 50001, and a simple blank was left where the old ignition switch had been.

Further changes occurred with the introduction of the CF/CR series in late 1972. A facelift was given to the dashboard and controls, principally by reinstating chromed bezels on all the dials and by using updated instrument faces in the style of the Dolo-mite and Triumph 2000/2.5 range, with the needles on the minor instruments now pivotting from the bottom rather than the top. As well as the introduction of the hand-operated dipswitch mentioned previously, the main head and sidelight switch was moved from the left of the steering column to the right of the dashboard, previously the home of the wiper switch, which was now combined with the screenwasher. Finally, the ammeter was deleted in favour of a volt-meter showing battery condition. The same matt-finish veneered dashboard continued, and the layout described above remained, with only minor detail alterations, until the end of TR6 production in 1976. North American specification TR6s had written instructions on most of the control knobs rather than the European symbol system, and post-CF1 cars had warning lights to indicate when various service operations were due.

CR/CF series TR6s had this slightly smaller steering wheel, with the word 'Triumph' on the horn push. The steering column lock can just be seen. A voltmeter has replaced the ammeter and the new light switch can be seen below the combined washer/wiper rocker switch. Notice that this car has tonneau fittings on the dash, even though it was built new with the factory hardtop. Chromed bezels have now reappeared on the instruments and the later 'Triumph Corporate' style of instrument faces has been introduced.

The TR4 'GTR Dove'

The Dove looks more elegant from the rear. Note the lack of a handle for the lift-up tailgate; this was released internally, allowing it to be lifted by inserting a finger into the depression below the tailgate. The vertical fuel filler cap can be seen on the tail.

David Bishop's unusual GTR4 Dove, with the height of the roof somewhat accentuated in this low-level shot.

Mention must be made of this rather curious model, which, although not factory inspired, was built in significant numbers.

The boot, rear deck, bulkhead and tonneau panels were removed from a standard TR4, and replaced by a full-length roof, moulded in glass-fibre and sweeping down to the rear of the car, where the original wings were adapted. This roof was sufficiently high above the rear axle to allow room for a bench seat giving 32in of headroom – enough for two reasonable-sized children, although adults could only be accommodated in great pain.

A top-hinged tailgate was fitted. In concept, the Dove was not unlike the MGB

GT, which it predated by around two years. The petrol tank had to be changed, to a flat 15-gallon tank that lived in the former spare wheel well. The spare wheel was repositioned on top of the tank, but sufficient space remained for luggage even with the rear seats occupied.

A wood rim steering wheel was fitted and many of the TR4 'extras' were normally incorporated. Opening rear quarter windows were added, and the side window glasses were also special as their top rear corners differed from standard TR4 items. The fuel filler cap was mounted on the rear panel below the tailgate, on the left-hand side. The whole car was fully trimmed, and

The front compartment of the Dove, clearly showing the painted door tops found on TR4s – but body paint should not normally be visible at the bottom of the door. The dashboard is correct, but the steering wheel and gearknob are not. The maplight is an addition, albeit from the appropriate period. Front footwells in TR4s were usually covered with rubber mats, but it is thought that Doves had carpet instead.

the conversion very professionally executed by coachbuilders Thomas Harrington and Co in West Sussex.

Although interested in the car and prepared to grant it a full factory warranty, Triumph did not see a large enough potential market to justify its taking over the model, so only limited production was achieved. Maybe the huge success of the MGB GT proved Triumph wrong? The Dove was inevitably considerably heavier than the basic TR4, so performance suffered as mechanically it was unaltered. It was also quite expensive, costing around 30 per cent more than a similarly equipped TR4. The car came with a very full and nicely-fitted tool kit, reputedly from the ambulances that Harrington also manufactured!

The car's name was derived from that of L.F. Dove and Co, Triumph distributors from Wimbledon, London, who were responsible for marketing it. In fact, the original literature refers to the car as a Dové, but for many years now the car has simply been called the Dove. The prototype, completed in 1963, was road tested by *Autocar* magazine, which approved.

Sales were steady throughout 1964–65, but controversy has always surrounded the number of Doves made. Dove's records do not appear to have survived, and the factory records in the care of the British Motor In-

Trim in the rear seat area was very neat, although poor headroom restricted the use of the seat to children. The back rest folded forwards to allow a longer luggage platform when the rear seats were not occupied. This car has the later TR4 front seats. The carpet is not original, but is very close to original specification. The door socket on the 'B' post should not have been painted.

The Dove's tailgate sat when closed on two black buffer pads. The luggage platform was rather high, because of the location of the petrol tank and spare wheel beneath it.

dustry Heritage Trust do not assist because Doves were made by converting standard cars delivered to Harrington, these being numbered in the ordinary 'CT' series. The best current estimate is that just under 100 TR4s were converted, together with a handful of TR4As. The TR4A Dove is as nearly mythical as a TR can get, but sales literature for TR4A Doves certainly existed. At least three TR4A-based Doves, believed to be original conversions, are known to have existed. Estimates of numbers are made more difficult because it was possible for an existing TR4 owner to present his car to Doves for an after-market conversion.

With hindsight, the Dove was a brave attempt to provide something both practical and different, but it did not quite succeed. The lines were not quite right, especially the somewhat heavy rear view. This, coupled with the extra cost and the widening choice of 'factory' coupés then becoming available from other manufacturers, prevented stronger sales.

This view of the Dove looking back towards the tailgate shows the luggage floor and spare wheel removed. The top of the flat petrol tank can be seen, and on this sat the spare wheel, fastened by the webbing straps seen. On the left-hand side is the impressive wooden framework holding the fitted tool kit, which came as standard with every Dove.

Production Changes

Significant changes by commission number (and engine or body number as appropriate).

CT 1
First production TR4, built on 18/7/61.

CT 2829
Rear springs changed from TR3A type to uprated 'non-handed' items.

CT 3434
Rear shock absorbers modified, and a different specification was introduced for US cars.

CT 4388 (disc wheels)
CT 4690 (wire wheels)
Steering geometry and top wishbone pressings changed, 16P front disc brake calipers introduced.

CT 5642 (body no)
Automatic boot lid stay replaces manual type.

CT 5656 (disc wheels)
CT 5783 (wire wheels)
Brake master cylinder reduced in bore from .075in to .070in.

CT 6344 (disc wheels)
CT 6389 (wire wheels)
Front upper wishbones again modified, as were top ball joints, steering tie-rod levers and bottom trunnions.

CT 6429
Bonnet panel slightly modified, incorporating a longer power bulge.

CT 7218
Trunnion to lower wishbone grease seals modified.

CT 7630 (wire wheels)
CT 7747 (disc wheels)
Front disc pads modified.

CT 9553
Backwards-pointing, TR3A type, radiator header tank deleted, integral header tank substituted.

CT 11479
Specification of rear shock absorbers changed again.

CT 14234 E
Open circuit engine breather/oil filler system replaced by new closed circuit type.

CT 15076 (body no)
New design of seats introduced.

CT 16800 E to CT 16900E
Trial batch of cars fitted with 175CD Stromberg carburettors.

CT 20064 (RHD), 20266 (LHD)
Steering rack and mountings modified, steering arms and chassis mounts for rack changed.

CT 20925 (body no)
Both seats now tip forward.

CT 21471 E
Stromberg 175CD carburettors now standard, on new inlet manifold and with slightly modified cylinder head.

CT 23383
Rear springs and axle check straps modified.

CT 29984
Front coil springs lengthened and previous packing pieces deleted.

CT 31506 (31636 overdrive)
Gearbox and clutch housing assembly modified.

CT 37689 (body no)
Bonnet panel again slightly modified.

CT 40304
Last TR4, built on 6/1/65.

CTC 50001
Introduction of TR4A. Modifications as detailed in text.

CTC 50125
Gearbox and clutch housing again modified slightly.

CTC 59836
Packing pieces changed on front coil springs.

CTC 62191
Stromberg carburettors deleted and twin SU Type HS6 1¾in instruments substituted, still on the same inlet manifold, needles type 'TW'.

CTC 62637
Temperature sender and gauge modified.

CTC 78684
Last TR4A, built 10/7/67.

CP1
First TR5 (prototype).

CD1
First TR250, built on 11/7/67.

CP2
First production TR5, built on 29/8/67.

CP 3101
Last TR5, built on 19/9/68.

CD 8594
Last TR250, built on 19/9/68.

Note. Very few production changes are recorded for the TR5/250 during its short life; those that have been found are referred to in the text.

CP 25001
First prototype TR6.

CC 25003
First carburettor TR6 found in records, built on 19/9/68.

CP 50001, CC 50001
First 1970 model cars, incorporating various changes including new design of disc wheel with 15 holes, deletion of previous Rostyle wheel trims, steering wheel changed from black finish and spokes with holes to anodised silver finish and spokes with slots, reclining mechanism fitted to seats. Windscreen surround now black irrespective of body colour. Chromed rocker cover replaced by silver painted item. New design of inlet manifold on carburettor cars, fuel tank changed, air collection manifold changed. Steering lock introduced on export cars.

CP 51163 (gearbox no), CC89817
Stronger Triumph Stag type internals fitted to gearbox.

CP 52420 E
Seven-blade plastic fan substituted for previous eight-blade fan, still of 12½in diameter.

CP 52786
Steering lock now standard on home-market cars (standard on export cars from CP/CC 50001).

CP 52868, CC 61571
Rear springs and rear wishbone support brackets uprated.

CP 53637, CC 63845
Pre-engaged starter motor fitted.

CP 53854
Gear lever knob modified.

CC 75001 E
Carburettor TR6's previous 'single downpipe' exhaust system replaced by 'twin throughout' system. New type inlet manifold on carburettor TR6s. Fuel tank on carburettor cars reduced to 10.25 gallons.

CR/CF1
First 1973 models, incorporating various changes, including derating injection engine to 125bhp, fitting 13-blade fan (14½in diameter), change of wheel centres from black to silver, change of steering wheel (reduction in diameter from 15in to 14½in), horn push changed from Triumph shield medallion to 'Triumph' lettering, non-USA seats fitted with head restraint facility, redesigned seat covers with coarser grain and fire resistant material, door and rear compartment trims redesigned, front grille fitted with chrome bead top and bottom, black front spoiler added below bumper, number plate illumination moved from top of rear bumper to underside of number plate recess, wiper arms changed from silver to black, heater intake flap changed to a fixed black plastic grille, more substantial front bumper mountings incorporated, fuel pump inertia cut-out switch fitted. Dashboard, instruments and switchgear updated, ammeter replaced by volt meter, dipswitch moved from floor to steering column, tunnel-mounted interior light deleted and two lights now fitted to shine into front footwells, commission plate moved from under bonnet to left-hand 'B' post. 'J' type overdrive introduced on 'CF' cars. New type of Stromberg carburettors on 'CF' cars, fuel tank on 'CF' cars now 9.5 gallons.

Note. It is believed that certain of the above changes were incorporated on some of the final CP/CC series cars, but it is not possible to be certain which changes came in earlier and when.

CR 567
'J' type overdrive unit introduced on CR series cars, to replace previous 'A' type.

CF 27001
Carburettor cars now had '5mph' protection, large, black, rubberised overriders front and rear, and repositioned front side/flasher lights transferred to beneath the front bumper. Also air injection fitted to engine exhaust to reduce emissions.

CR 6701
Last TR6 (P1), built on 7/2/75.

CF 58328
Last carburettor TR6, built on 15/7/76.

Notes
1. 'L', 'O' and 'U' suffixes have been omitted to avoid confusion.
2. Because of the multitude of small changes – particularly on US cars – that took place during the 15-year production run of these cars, this list cannot be exhaustive. It seeks only to detail the more significant changes where the change point is known.
3. Specification changes consequent upon the introduction of each successive model are dealt with in the text and are *not* included in this list, which details only changes that occurred during the production run of the particular model itself.
4. The cataloguing of actual production changes in the Parts Manuals becomes less precise beyond the TR4A, and there are frequent references to changes but with blanks as to the actual change point. For this reason it is more difficult to be accurate for the later cars, so less information can be included.

OPTIONS, EXTRAS & ACCESSORIES

With the passage of time and the growing expectations of the motoring public, standard cars as supplied by Triumph inevitably became better equipped, leading to a change in the type of options available. Since fewer cars were being used in competition, many of the previously available competition-orientated items were also deleted – and more comfort and safety options became listed.

The following items were listed for the TR4. Except where noted, most continued for the TR4A. It seems likely that several options and accessories referred to in the TR2/3/3A section might have been available also for TR4/4As, but I cannot find any references to confirm. Some of the following items may well have been changed or deleted during the car's run from 1961-67, but details have not been established.

Aluminium oil sump kit. Including the 16 longer set screws required to fit it to the crankcase. Not specifically listed for the TR4A, but still available.

Competition sparking plugs.

Lightened Flywheel. Including ring-gear. Not specifically listed for the TR4A, but still available.

Competition shock absorbers. Believed to have been available, but I can find no specific details.

Starting handle kit. Deleted for the TR4A.

Two-speed windscreen wiper kit. Including switch, motor and wiring. Standard on the TR4A.

Continental touring kit. Including cylinder head gasket, fan belt, sparking plug, set of hoses, distributor cover, rotor arm, condensor, contact set, water pump seal, petrol pump diaphragm, oil and petrol flexible pipes, inlet and exhaust valves, valve spring set, rocker cover gasket and a set of spare bulbs.

Fog lamp. Part no 501702 – later sealed beam type 569908 substituted.

Spot lamp. Part no 501703 – later sealed beam type 569907 offered.

Wing mirror. Part no 502459.

Reversing light kit.

Tonneau cover. Either left- or right-hand drive, including studs and fixing brackets for facia. Available in black or white.

Safety harness kit. In either two-point or three-point fixing for TR4. Lap/diagonal three-point fixing type for TR4A.

Electric screen defroster. Suction type to be mounted on inside of windscreen.

Anti-mist panel. Apparently for the backlight of the Surrey hard top.

Surrey hardtop conversion set. Available in black or white. This appears not to have been a full kit to convert a roadster into a Surrey top car, but merely the parts necessary to provide the 'soft' centre section, which was not usually supplied with a car equipped with the Surrey hardtop from new, unless specially ordered.

'Power-Stop' vacuum brake servo kit.

Wood rim steering wheel. Part no 307245.

'Speed' mirrors. Part no 573677.

Wing mirror – 'D' type 'fly-back'. Part no 560632.

Wing mirror – 'Turina' type 'fly-back'. Part no 570409.

Wing mirror – round, rigid. Part no 608467/WL.

Wing mirror – 'Morgan' type. Part no 608467/M.

Wheel rim finisher. Part no 502160.

Overdrive. Officially available on new cars only, though in practice a 'retro-fit' conversion was available from the factory.

Wire wheels. For TR4, either 48- or 60-spoke wheels, finishes as detailed in 'Wheels & Tyres' section. Only 60-spoke wheels for TR4A.

4.1 to 1 rear axle ratio. Only with overdrive option, and when ordered from new.

Occasional rear seat cushion.

Leather upholstery.

Touch-in paint. In ¼-pint tins.

Heater. Fresh air type, 'retro-fit' conversion possible.

Hard top. With steel (or aluminium) centre section, normally ordered with a new car, but could be 'retro fitted'. Surrey soft centre section was normally 'extra' to the hardtop itself.

Goodyear white wall tyres. Crossply 5.90 × 15.

Goodyear 'Motorway Special' tyres. Replaced by Dunlop SP radial tyres for TR4A.

Michelin X radial tyres.

Radio. See TR3/3A options list for details.

Push button radio. See TR3/3A options list for details.

Windscreen washer kit. Including dashboard plunger knob, piping and bottle – manual operation. Standard on TR4A.

In the official parts manual, only the following options are listed for the TR5. Where appropriate, extra details are given in the TR4/4A list above. A heater was now standard.

Door mirror. Passenger side to match the standard item on the driver's side. Part no 622352.

Safety harness kit. Two- or three- point fixing, or lap/diagonal type.

Electric screen defroster.

Anti-mist panel. For backlight of Surrey hardtop only.

Touch-in paint.

'Surrey' centre section canopy. In black or white.

Oil cooler kit. Part no 308367.

Skid plate. Part no 308208 (fitted under radiator/sump area).

Continental touring kit. Containing parts largely as before.

Wire Wheels. 60-spoke with octagonal safety caps.

Overdrive.

Radio. Push-button or standard type.

Tonneau Cover.

Michelin XAS radial tyres.

Hardtop. Surrey type as before.

Leather upholstery. Believed to have been available on the TR5, but rarely specified.

The rear lines of the TR6, especially with the hard top fitted, give the car a purposeful and uncompromising look, accentuated by the matt black rear panel. The British Leyland logo of this CR series car can be seen at the base of the front wing.

The following options were listed for the TR6.

Tonneau cover. Standard from the start of 1974. Several types, to take account of LHD or RHD, and whether or not head-rests were fitted.

Wire wheels. 72-spoke with octagonal safety nuts – deleted from May 1973.

Overdrive. Originally 'A' type on top three gears, then 'J' type on third and top only from car nos CR567, CF1, late 1972. From December 1973, overdrive became standard.

Radio. Various types and styles.

Safety harness. Static variety (standard after May 1972) and 'automatic' inertia reel type. 'Audible warning' type fitted for some markets.

Steering wheel glove. In leather or simu-lated leather. Wood rim wheel no longer available.

Door buffer. Sold in pairs. Made of rub-ber, with or without reflectors.

Safety warning triangle.

Passenger door mirror.

Wing mirrors. Long or short arm – convex type.

Exterior driving mirror. Fitted as stan-dard after car CF1 for USA – possibly also standard on 'CR' cars.

Continental touring kit. Two types, for

These substantial hard top fixing bolts picked up on the hood stick fixing points. A hard top car could be converted to a roadster and vice versa, the factory producing kits for this purpose.

PI or carburettor cars. Contents largely as before.

Electric screen defroster.

Anti-mist backlight. For hardtop rear sc-reen.

Hardtop. The TR6 one-piece type.

Headrests. Adjustable type. Standard on North American cars, optional on later cars for other markets.

Touch-in paint.

Towing attachment kit.

Oil cooler kit.

Steering column lock. Standard from car no CP 52786. Evidently this item was also available as an option as far back as

the TR4A. However, I can find no specific mention in any published literature.

Skid plate.

Hardtop to softtop conversion kit. Included everything necessary to con-vert a car built with the factory hardtop into an open roadster. There were two types: 'USA' and 'everywhere else'.

IDENTIFICATION, DATING & PRODUCTION FIGURES

As with the earlier cars, Triumph used a logical numerical series of commission numbers with alphabetical prefixes and suffices to identify these vehicles, each particular series having its own two-letter prefix. The letter 'L' to denote a left-hand drive car and 'O' to denote a car with overdrive as an original factory fitment continued to be used, although for some reason the left-hand drive suffix was changed to 'U' in late 1971. For an explanation of the term 'commission number', please see the TR2/3/3A section.

The TR4 prefix was 'CT', and the first production car, CT1, was built on 18/7/61. The series then continued as a straight numerical run through to CT 40304 built on 6/1/65. To assist with dating, the first car built in 1962 was CT 2649 on 1/1/62, the first in 1963 is believed to have been CT 18605 (not verifiable as production microfilm record is missing), the first in 1964 was CT 28709 on 1/1/64, and the first in 1965 was CT 40193 on 1/1/65.

The TR4A prefix was 'CTC'. Rigid rear axle North American cars still had the prefix 'CT', but they were numbered in the same sequence as the 'CTC' cars. The first TR4A was CTC 50001: since CTC 50001 to 50005 were prototypes and development cars, the first true production TR4A was CTC 50006 built on 5/1/65. The first car in 1966 was CTC 64148 built on 3/1/66, and in 1967 it was CTC 75172 built on 2/1/67. The final TR4A was CTC 78684 built either on 10/7/67 or 17/7/67, the uncertainty being due to a contradiction in the factory records. I am aware that these dates are somewhat earlier than the previously quoted date for the end of four-cylinder TR production, but nevertheless the records do definitely indicate that TR4A production ceased in July 1967.

Some cars were still being exported from Coventry as kits for local assembly, and these frequently had an extra local prefix letter; for instance, Belgian-assembled TR4As had 'ICTC' prefixes. Belgian assembly continued right through TR6 production. No cars were built with commission numbers between 40305 and 50000 inclusive. Although North American cars were numbered in the above series, they were sometimes given an additional plate by the importer, bearing the letters 'STC' (Standard-Triumph Corporation)

The TR4/4A type of commission plate, mounted on the front inner bulkhead. This one, from Ken Westwood's car, shows 56 for Royal Blue paint, 16 for Midnight Blue trim and an 'O' for overdrive at the extreme end of the 'CTC' number. Were the car trimmed in leather, an 'H' would prefix the trim number.

CR/CF series TR6s had the commission plate on the door 'B' post. The plates were produced by British Metal Engraving Ltd and came ready numbered in commission number sequence. However, details of paint and trim colour, and whether overdrive was fitted, were added at the factory by hand-stamping.

followed by the last two digits of the model year. On the paperwork for a North American car, therefore, a commission number may appear in full as, for instance, 'STC 67 CTC 70001 LO'.

The manufacturer's name on the commission plate was given as 'Standard Motor Company Limited' on TR4s, but was changed to 'Standard-Triumph Motor Company Limited' on TR4As and subsequent cars built up to the end of 1970. From January 1971 to the end of the CP series of TR6s, 'Triumph Motor Company Limited' was used. All CR/CF series TR6s had the maker's name rendered as 'Triumph Motors, British Leyland UK Limited'.

TR5s were numbered in the 'CP' series, starting with CP1 as a prototype. The first production car in the records is CP2, dated 29/8/67. The first in 1968 is CP 586 built on 1/1/68, and the last TR5 is CP 3101, built on 19/9/68. As far as can be established for certain, only 2947 genuine TR5s were built

although the numbering was to 3101. It is not certain where the gaps in the numerical sequence fall. In view of the rarity and value of the TR5, cases have been known of 'converting' TR250 carburettor cars into supposedly genuine TR5s, so a check with the British Motor Industry Heritage Trust against the commission number would be a wise precaution prior to parting with a large bag of gold for one of these cars.

Some TR5s were assembled from Completely Knocked Down (CKD) kits in Belgium, and these cars have both an 'I' prefix and a 'P' suffix in addition to the normal LHD suffix: for example, ICP 500-LP. The North American TR250s had their own sequence, based on a 'CD' prefix and an 'L' suffix. The first TR250 was CD1-L built on 11/7/67, the first in 1968 was CD 2685-L, and the last was CD 8594-L built on 19/9/68. Again, there must be some gaps as only 8484 TR250s are believed to have been made.

The TR6 injection cars were numbered as follows, based on CP and CR prefixes:

1968 First car, CP 25001, believed to be prototype. CP 25002 to CP 25145 were CKD kits. First built-up car was CP 25146, built on 28/11/68.

1969 First car in year, CP 25159, built on 2/1/69. Last '1969' model, CP 26998, believed built on 10/9/69. First '1970' model, CP 50001, built on 1/9/69 (CP 50002 to CP 50436 were believed to be mainly CKD cars).

1970 First car in year, CP 50465, built on 1/1/70.

1971 First car in year, CP 52786, built on 1/1/71. Last '1971' model, CP 54572, built on 7/9/71 (CP 54573 to CP 54584 were CKD cars). First '1972' model, CP 75001, built on 27/9/71.

1972 First car in year, CP 75455, built on 3/1/72. Last '1972' model, CP 77718, built on 21/9/72. First built-up '1973' model, CR 169, built on 15/11/72 (CR 1 to CR 168 were CKD cars).

1973 First car in year, CR 665, built on 2/1/73. Last '1973' model, CR 2911, built on 17/10/73. First built-up '1974' model, CR 5049, built on 14/9/73 (CR 5001 to 5048 were CKD cars).

1974 First car in year, CR 5613, built on 1/1/74.

1975 First car in year, CR 6631, built on 1/1/75. Last injection car, CR 6701, built on 7/2/75.

The TR6 carburettor models again had their own numbering series, prefixed CC and then CF. They are numbered and dated as follows:

1968 First car, CC 25003 L, built on 19/9/68 (25001 and 25002 not found in records).

1969 First car in year, CC 27384 L, built on 2/1/69. Last '1969' model, CC 32142 L, built on 19/12/69. First '1970' model, CC 50001 L, built on 22/11/69.

1970 First car in year, CC 51033 L, built on 1/1/70.

1971 First car in year, CC 60903 L, built on 1/1/71. Last '1971' model, CC 67893 L, built on 20/8/71. First '1972' model, CC 75001 L, built on 20/8/71.

1972 First car in year, CC 78813 U, built on 3/1/72. Last '1972' model, CC 85737 U, built on 5/10/72. First '1973' model, CF 1 U, built on 11/9/72.

1973 First car in year, CF 4029 U, built on 2/1/73.

1974 First car in year, CF 17002 U, built on 2/1/74. Last '1974' model, CF 25777 U, built on 18/9/74. First '1975' model, CF 27002 U, built on 22/8/74.

1975 First car in year, CF 29581 U, built on 2/1/75. Last '1975' model, CF 39991 U, built on 23/8/75. First '1976' model, CF 50001 U, built on 29/8/75.

1976 First car in year, CF 52315 U, built on 5/1/76. Last TR6 of all, CF 58328 U, built on 15/7/76.

The commission plates on TR4 and TR4A models were riveted to the bulkhead/scuttle panel under the bonnet adjacent to the windscreen wiper motor. On TR5, TR250 and CP/CC TR6 models, the plate was riveted to the front wheel arch top (usually the nearside on RHD cars), again under the bonnet. CR/CF series TR6s had the plate riveted to the 'B' post on the left-hand side, visible when the door was opened.

Engine numbers on TR4s and TR4As have the 'CT' prefix and an 'E' suffix, factory rebuilt engines having an 'FRE' suffix. The number is stamped on the left-hand side of the block. Engines prefixed 'CTA' indicate that they are to 1991cc specification.

TR5 engine numbers are prefixed 'CP' and suffixed either 'E' or 'HE'. TR250 engines are prefixed 'CC' (not 'CD' as expected) and suffixed 'E'. On TR6s of all types, the engine number prefix follows the commission number prefix – CP, CC, CR or CF. The suffix is 'HE' on injection cars; carburettor cars have either 'HE' or 'E' up to late 1971, and 'UE' thereafter. It is possible that some Californian specification cars had engines that were suffixed 'UCE', but this is not certain.

As regards body numbers, unlike the

PRODUCTION FIGURES

	TR4	TR4A	TR5	TR250	TR6PI	TR6 Carb	Total
1961	2470						2470
1962	15933						15933
1963	10082						10082
1964	11518						11518
1965	250	13735					13985
1966		11097					11097
1967		3633	150	2357			6140
1968			2797	6127	51	1468	10443
1969					2053	6632	8685
1970					2401	9702	12103
1971					2681	10810	13491
1972					2674	10766	13440
1973					2901	11924	14825
1974					1072	11440	12512
1975					79	9113	9192
1976						6083	6083
Total	40253	28465	2947	8484	13912	77938	171999

Notes
1. The year totals are based on cars built, not cars delivered in any particular year.
2. The split in 1971 between injection and carburettor cars has had to be based on chassis numbers rather than Triumph Production Statistics, as for this one year only Triumph counted the two models together.

sidescreen cars, each body had only one number, usually found on a plate fixed in the scuttle/bulkhead area under the bonnet. These were in all cases in numerical series roughly equivalent to the relevant commission number, and carried a suffix rather than a prefix. TR4 and TR4A bodies carried a 'CT suffix, TR5s a 'CP' suffix, TR250s a 'CC' suffix and TR6s of both types carried the same suffix as the relevant commission number prefix. Rear axles and gearboxes of all cars also carried serial numbers in numerical sequence, again usually with a similar prefix to that appropriate to the particular car.

The accompanying production figures have been drawn from factory records held by the British Motor Industry Heritage Trust. Not all these figures agree with those previously published, and one cannot assume that all numerical sequences are necessarily unbroken – certain gaps do exist and so there are some discrepancies in totals. As I said in the TR2/3/3A/3B section, one cannot pin down any gaps without going through over 170,000 individual records, which no-one has yet had the time or inclination to do!

It is possible with reasonable accuracy to split home market and export cars as shown in the second table, although again there are a few discrepancies. As previously, the huge majority (90–95 per cent) of TRs were exported, and most of those exported were built with left-hand drive. All the carburettor TR250s and TR6s were exported, almost all to North America, although there were some 'personal export' deliveries elsewhere, principally to servicemen.

PRODUCTION DESTINATIONS

	Home	Export	CKD
TR4			
1961	10	2448	12
1962	964	14309	660
1963	796	9142	144
1964	819	10657	42
1965	3	247	0
TR4A			
1965	1073	11714	948
1966	1000	8993	1104
1967	1002	2079	552
TR5 PI			
1967	25	29	96
1968	1136	1661	n/a
TR6 PI			
1968	0	51	n/a
1969	704	461	888
1970	1308	1093	n/a
1971	1288	1393	n/a
1972	1720	954	n/a
1973	2002	899	n/a
1974	826	246	n/a
1975	41	38	n/a

Notes
1. TR250 and TR6 carburettor cars were all exported. As far as can be ascertained, none was built as a CKD kit – thus the totals are as given in the 'Production Figures' table.
2. Where CKD figures are given as n/a (not available), CKD cars built that year are included within the export total.

COLOUR SCHEMES

As was the case with the earlier cars, colour and trim combinations are complex and varied. From TR4 number CT 28807, built on 3/1/64, the different paint colours were each given a two or three digit code number which appeared on the car's commission number plate, the numbering being extended as new colours arrived. Also on the plate was a separate two digit number indicating the trim colour. This colour numbering system continued through to the end of TR6 production, the colour numbers used on the TR4–6 range being as follows (note that some colours are paint only, some are trim only and some colours are for both paint and trim):

11	Black
12	Matador Red
13	Light Tan
16	Midnight Blue
17	Damson
19	New White
23	Siena Brown
25	Triumph Racing Green (Conifer)
26	Wedgwood Blue
27	Shadow Blue
32	Signal Red
33	New Tan
34	Jasmine Yellow
54	Saffron Yellow
55	Laurel Green
56	Royal Blue
63	Chestnut
64	Mimosa Yellow
65	Emerald Green
66	Valencia Blue
72	Pimento Red
73	Maple Beige
74	Beige
75	British Racing Green (1975)
82	Carmine Red
84	Topaz Yellow
85	Java Green
92	Magenta
93	Russet Brown
94	Inca Yellow
96	Sapphire Blue
106	Mallard Blue
126	French Blue
136	Delft Blue
146	Tahiti Blue

Those few colours used on TR4s prior to 1964 and deleted by that date do not have a number – Spa White, Powder Blue, pre-1964 British Racing Green and Velasquez Cream. I have not attempted to give paint manufacturers' references for the paints for these later cars, unlike the earlier cars, because matching paints for the TR4–6

series are more readily available from commercial sources simply because the cars are more recent. Virtually all the above paint colours are still listed by the major manufacturers.

Full details of paint, trim and hood colour combinations for each model are given in the accompanying tables.

TRIUMPH TR4 COLOURS

Paint	Trim
Spa White[1]	Black, Red[8]
Powder Blue[2]	Midnight Blue[9], Black
British Racing Green[3]	Black, Red[8]
Black	Black, (Matador) Red[8]
Signal Red	Black, (Matador) Red[8]
Velasquez Cream[4]	Black, Red[8]
New White[5]	Black, Matador Red[8]
Wedgwood Blue[6]	Midnight Blue[9]
Triumph Racing Green[7]	Black⋅

Notes to table
1. Spa White was available only up to CT 21495, in March 1963.
2. Powder Blue was available only up to CT 20916, in March 1963.
3. British Racing Green was available only up to CT 19518, in January 1963.
4. Velasquez Cream was found only on a small number of cars in 1961.
5. New White was available only from CT 21520, in March 1963.
6. Wedgwood Blue was available only from CT 21247, in March 1963.
7. Triumph Racing Green (also called Conifer Green) was available only from CT 19521, in January 1963. Triumph Racing Green *may* be the same colour as British Racing Green.
8. It is uncertain whether red trim was Matador Red from the start of production, or whether the red trim colour was changed. An American sales brochure dated October 1961 indicates that Spa White was also available with blue trim in addition to Red and Black.
9. It is uncertain whether blue trim was Midnight Blue from the start of production, or whether the blue trim colour was changed.

General notes
Hoods were available in black or white for all colour schemes, with the possible exception of Velasquez Cream where only black may have been offered; tonneau covers usually matched hood colour. Surrey top hoods were also available in black or white. Hard tops could be specified in black, white or body colour. Trim could be in Vynide or leather; if in leather, the trim code number on 1964–65 cars is prefixed 'H' on the commission plate, prior to the colour number.

TRIUMPH TR4A COLOURS

Paint	Trim
Black	Black, Matador Red
New White	Black, Matador Red
Triumph Racing Green	Black
Wedgwood Blue	Midnight Blue
Signal Red	Black, Matador Red
Royal Blue[1]	Black, Midnight Blue

Notes to table
1. Royal Blue was a new colour, believed to have been introduced in March 1966 from approximately CTC 67685.

General notes
Hoods were available in black or white for all colour schemes; tonneau covers always matched hood colour. Surrey top hoods were available in black or white. Hard tops could be specified in black, white or body colour. Trim could be Ambla or leather; if in leather, an 'H' prefix appears before the colour number on the commission plate.

It appears that during the last months of TR4A production, the TR5 colour Valencia Blue (probably with Tan trim) was available, and several such cars are known to exist, although this colour was not officially listed for the TR4A.

TRIUMPH TR5/250 COLOURS

Paint	Trim
New White	Black, Matador Red
Triumph Racing Green	Black, Light Tan
Signal Red	Black
Jasmine Yellow	Black
Royal Blue	Black, Shadow Blue[1]
Valencia Blue	Black, Light Tan

Notes to table
1. Midnight Blue trim may have been used on some Royal Blue cars.

General notes
TR5 and TR250 models are believed to have shared the same colour range; the colour of the TR250's nose stripes is described in the 'Bodies & Body Trim' section. Hoods were now predominantly black, but some cars with white hoods have been found in factory records; white *may* have been available with all colour schemes. Tonneau covers always matched hood colour. Hard tops could be specified in black, white or body colour. Trim was almost always in Ambla; leather now very rare. Black may have continued to be available as a paint colour.

TRIUMPH TR6 COLOURS (CC/CP series, by model year)

Paint	Trim 1968–69	Trim 1969–70	Trim 1970–71	Trim 1971–72
Damson	Black Light Tan	Black New Tan[1]	Black New Tan	Black New Tan
New White	Black Matador Red Light Tan	Black Matador Red New Tan[1]	Black Matador Red New Tan	Black Matador Red New Tan Shadow Blue[2]
Triumph Racing Green[3]	Black Light Tan Matador Red?			
Signal Red	Black Light Tan	Black New Tan[1]	Black New Tan	
Jasmine Yellow	Black Light Tan	Black New Tan[1]	Black New Tan	Black New Tan
Royal Blue[4]	Black Shadow Blue	Black Shadow Blue	Black Shadow Blue	
Siena Brown		Black New Tan[5]	Black New Tan	Black New Tan
Laurel Green		Black New Tan[1] Matador Red?	Black New Tan[6]	Black
Saffron Yellow			Black New Tan	Black New Tan
Sapphire Blue[4]			Black Shadow Blue	Black Shadow Blue
Pimento Red				Black New Tan
Emerald Green				Black

Notes to table
1. New Tan replaces Light Tan early in 1970, so earlier cars in 1969–70 model year would instead have had Light Tan.
2. Shadow Blue trim might have been offered for New White cars before the 1971–72 model year.
3. Triumph Racing Green was often referred to as Conifer Green.
4. Royal Blue appears to have been replaced by Sapphire Blue early in 1971, so both colours were used in the 1970–71 model year.
5. Siena Brown appears to have been introduced early in 1970, so may never have been found with Light Tan trim.
6. New Tan trim may have been offered for Laurel Green cars into the 1971–72 model year.

General notes
It is believed that fuel injection and carburettor cars were always available in the same colours. Hoods and tonneau covers (if fitted) were normally black, but white was found on a few early cars in 1968–69. Hard tops were normally painted body colour; black or white may also have been available on all cars, but possibly only with Triumph Racing Green.

TRIUMPH TR6 COLOURS (CF/CR series, by model year)

Paint	Trim 1972–73	Trim 1973–74	Trim 1974–75	Trim 1975–76	Trim 1976[1]
New White	Black Chestnut Shadow Blue	Black Chestnut Shadow Blue	Black Chestnut Shadow Blue	Black Chestnut	Black Beige
Siena Brown	Black New Tan				
Mimosa Yellow	Black Chestnut	Black Chestnut	Black Chestnut	Black Chestnut Beige	
Emerald Green	Black	Black			
Pimento Red	Black Chestnut	Black Chestnut	Black Chestnut	Black Chestnut	Black
Carmine Red	Black New Tan	Black New Tan	Black Beige[2]	Beige	Beige
Magenta	Black	Black			
Sapphire Blue	Black Shadow Blue	Black Shadow Blue			
Mallard Blue	Black New Tan	Black New Tan			
French Blue	Black	Black	Black	Black	
Maple		Black New Tan	Black Beige[2]	Beige	
British Racing Green (1975)			Black Beige[2]	Black Beige	Beige
Topaz Yellow			Black	Black Beige	
Java Green			Black	Black	Black
Delft Blue			Black Shadow Blue	Black Beige	
Russet Brown					Beige
Inca Yellow					Black
Tahiti Blue					Black Beige

Notes to table
1. The last column indicates colours in use towards the end of production in July 1976; CF (North American carburettor) models had an altered and reduced range in the last few months. Of these colours, Russet Brown, Inca Yellow and Tahiti Blue were also used on MGBs and MG Midgets. However, Mallard Blue is *not* the same colour as MG's Green Mallard, nor does it appear that the TR6's British Racing Green matches any similar MG/BMC colours. The TR6's Carmine Red *may* be the same as MG's Carmine Red.
2. Beige seems to have been introduced gradually during 1975.

General notes
The trim colours listed may not be exhaustive. Carpet colours matched trim, except New Tan carpet was supplied with Chestnut and Beige trim. Hoods and tonneau covers were probably always in black, but white may have been possible as a special order. Hard tops were always body colour from 1973 model year onwards.

Buying Guide

From most points of view, the TR lover who wishes to possess an original car in excellent condition would be best advised to try to find a derelict but original car, needing total overhaul but – and this is the vital bit – complete in every detail. Beware the dismantled or partly dismantled car. It is so difficult to check that everything is present with this type of purchase, and one can almost guarantee that some parts will have been 'liberated' – and, in the nature of things, these will be the items that are hardest to find!

Purchasing a derelict but complete and original TR is perhaps the best way of ensuring that one ends up with a thoroughly sound and original car, whether one does the job oneself or employs reputable professionals. However, do not underestimate the cost of a total rebuild, which can frequently exceed the value of the completed car. At least with this approach one pays only the minimum price for the car in the first place: it is all too easy to pay thousands more for an ostensibly better car, only to find that it still needs a full rebuild once one has looked beyond a shiny coat of paint and new upholstery.

Undoubtedly the most cost-effective, but probably not the most satisfying, way of acquiring an excellent TR is to purchase an already completely and correctly rebuilt car. The price will be high, but this is the route for someone who has neither the time nor inclination to become involved in restoration. Obviously, one must be sure that the car is what it purports to be. Before parting with a considerable bag of gold, check, or have an expert check, that the car really is to original specification – use this book! – and is in top condition. Most fully rebuilt cars will have had photographs taken during the process, and a set of these should be passed on with the car.

Occasionally there appear on the market genuine, low-mileage, low-ownership TRs that have never needed restoration, having been cherished and properly maintained throughout their lives. Such cars exist and are usually known to the clubs, but their value, because of their rarity, is very much a matter of conjecture. If you can find one and can afford it, buy it!

Be particularly careful of the cars that inhabit the middle ground between the restoration projects at one end and the rebuilt or totally original cars at the other. It is all too easy to pay too much for a car that is running and looks smart, yet in reality needs a lot of work. Inspect such a car thoroughly, enquire why it is for sale and accept that it will need more maintenance than a fully rebuilt car – and that ultimately it too will need a major restoration. This is not to say that such 'middling' cars should be altogether shunned – after all, it depends on what one wants and can afford. I merely advise special caution.

As a breed, TRs are robust and rugged in the extreme. Having a strong, separate chassis frame gives a TR a considerable advantage over such cars as MGBs and Jaguar E-types with their monocoque construction, in terms of both ease of rebuild and maintenance. TR engines are equally robust, especially the four-cylinder units, although these can suffer crankshaft breakage; the six-cylinder engines can develop excessive crankshaft end-float. As ever, corrosion is the main enemy, and its extent should always be investigated thoroughly. In assessing a car, pay particular attention to originality of specification and to what extras are fitted – overdrive and wire wheels, for instance, will significantly increase a car's value.

Research the subject thoroughly before buying any TR; read all the books, join the clubs, go to meetings and talk to experienced owners. They are usually only too ready to dispense their hard-won advice, and thereby prevent others from repeating errors they may themselves have made. Having done this research, buy cautiously, never on impulse. Do not be afraid to reject cars and be prepared for wasted journeys. A lot of TRs were made, a lot have survived, and the choice is usually good.

As to where to buy, the classic car magazines carry plenty of advertisements from dealers and individuals, and some hours studying these will give a good idea of asking prices and availability. The classified columns of club magazines generally have cars for sale at slightly lower figures, but these tend to be snapped up quickly. There *are* reputable dealers in TRs, but I have to say there are at least as many who are not – and the same applies to restoration firms. One must be cynical and expect to encounter the 'fast buck and tosh it up' brigade! I have always found it preferable to deal with enthusiasts, and particularly other club members. There is no doubt that one will pay less for a given car this way, if only because the vendor will not have overheads to support. However, there is no recourse to a private individual, whereas a reputable dealer with a good name to protect should be anxious to keep a customer happy.

Most TRs, except fuel-injected cars, went to the USA, and recently a large number of such cars have been reimported to the UK and elsewhere in Europe. Some of these cars have been converted to right-hand drive for sale in the UK; one should be aware of this when purchasing and ensure that the conversion has been carried out correctly. Be certain that the paperwork is in order and that all duties have been paid. Because the TR manufactured with right-hand drive is the true rarity, bear in mind that the value in the UK of an imported car, however well restored and converted, will never be quite the same as that of an original right-hand drive car in equivalent condition. It is true that cars imported from some parts of the USA are indeed amazingly rust-free, but it is a large country with all types of climates. I have seen cars from North America that are as evilly corroded as anything native found in Britain. Do not believe the claims of some vendors!

You may feel that I have been unnecessarily cynical in this section, but I have seen some disasters. It is so easy to end up with the wrong car altogether, or the right car for which one has paid too much, or, even worse, a disastrous combination of the two! As is so often said, you tend generally to get what you pay for. Decide what you can afford and what you want the car for – be sure, in fact, that you really want an old car at all, no matter how good its condition. Fantasy rarely lives up to reality, and too many people have lost a lot of cash by finding out too late that they really feel happier in their 'Eurobox GTi'.

I hasten to add that the sheer practicality and fun of any TR makes it a better bet for modern motoring than most of its contemporaries, and if, having considered the negative points I have mentioned, you really do want to embark upon classic sports car ownership, then the TR is an excellent choice. Come and join us!

Clubs

The principal TR club, catering for all models of TR, is the TR Register, founded in 1970. This club is professionally run by a general manager, Rosy Good, and staff, responsible to a volunteer committee elected from the membership, which numbers approximately 7000. The club's full-time office is at 271 High Street, Berkhamsted, Hertfordshire HP4 1AA (tel: 0442-865906). The club publishes its magazine *TRaction* eight times annually.

There is also the smaller TR Drivers Club, founded in 1980, which again caters for all models of TR. The contact address is the Membership Secretary, TR Drivers Club, 39 Brook Street, Benson, Oxfordshire.

The USA has several clubs catering for TRs, one of the principal ones being the Triumph Register of America. The contact is Joe Richards, 5650 Brook Road N W, Lancaster, Ohio 42130. In addition, there is the Triumph Register of Southern California; contact Martin Lodawer, 20929 Lassen St. #112 Chatsworth, California 91311.

Offshoots of the TR Register and clubs affiliated to it exist in at least 20 other countries, including Austria, Australia, Belgium, Canada, France, Germany, Holland, Hong Kong, Ireland, Italy, Japan, New Zealand, Norway, Portugal, South Africa, Spain, Sweden and Switzerland. As addresses change relatively frequently, contact is best made via the TR Register office.

The badge of the original TR club, the Triumph Sports Owners' Association, formed by the company itself in 1954 and in existence, it is believed, until the early 1960s. The other badge, part of which can be seen on the grille behind, is not original.

Specialists

The following information is believed to be accurate as at April 1991. Neither the author nor the publishers will be held liable nor responsible for any errors or omissions or the consequences thereof. The inclusion of a firm within this list does not in any way imply a recommendation, nor does the exclusion of any firm imply any criticism. By its very nature such a list cannot be exhaustive, and there are doubtless reputable restorers and suppliers not included. If in any doubt, prospective customers should contact the TR Register office or other TR clubs for up to date information, or alternatively look in current issues of club publications or the specialist classic car press.

Cox and Buckles Spares (a division of Moss Motors), 22/28 Manor Road, Richmond, Surrey TW9 1YB (tel: 081-948 6666). *TR parts suppliers, workshop and restoration facilities.*

Moss Special Tuning and Triumphtune, 22/28 Manor Road, Richmond, Surrey TW9 1YB, (tel: 081-948 6668). *TR tuning and competition parts.*

Cox and Buckles Spares Midlands, 991 Wolverhampton Road, Oldbury, W. Midlands B69 4RT (tel: 021-544 5555). *Comprehensive TR parts suppliers.*

Revington TR Spares, Home Farm, Middlezoy, Somerset TA7 0PD (tel: 0823 69437). *Spares, both supply and manufacture, workshop facilities and restoration work.*

Northern TR Centre, Sedgefield Industrial Estate, Sedgefield, Cleveland (tel: 0740 21447). *Cars for sale, restoration work and workshop facilities.*

Racetorations, Sandars Road, Gainsborough, Lincs DN21 1RZ (tel: 0427 616565). *Restoration, parts, workshop facilities, competition parts and preparation.*

TR Bitz, Unit 3G Lyncastle Way, Barley Castle Trading Estate, Appleton, Warrington, Cheshire WA4 4SN (tel: 0925 861861). *Spares, restoration and workshop facilities.*

TR GB, 3 Warners Drove, Somersham, Huntingdon, Cambs PE17 3HW (tel: 0487 842168). *Parts and restoration.*

TR Shop, 16 Chiswick High Road, London W4 1TH (tel: 081-995 6621). *Parts suppliers.*

Protek Engineering, Unit 13, Bushells Business Park, Hithercroft, Wallingford, Oxford (tel: 0491 32372). *Restorations, spares, cars for sale, workshop and engineering facilities.*

Chestnut House Sports Cars, Tydd St Giles, Wisbech, Cambs PE13 5NU (tel: 0945 870833). *Restoration work and workshop facilities.*

M. E. and J. W. Pumford, 86/90 Seaview Road, Liscard, Wallasey, Merseyside L45 4LB (tel: 051-638 6060). *Restoration work, TR fuel-injection specialists.*

T and M Classics, Waterlands Farm, Chinnor Road, Thame, Oxford OX9 3RE (tel: 0844 261712). *Restorations and spares.*

TR Enterprises, Dale Lane, Blidworth, Notts NG21 0SA (tel: 0623 793807). *Parts, restorations, competitions preparation, workshop facilities.*

Martin's Fuel Injection, Unit 6B, Parsonage Farm Estate, Stansted, Essex (tel: 0279 816587). *TR fuel-injection specialist.*

Rimmer Brothers, 115 Lincoln Road, Branston, Lincoln LN4 1PX (tel: 0522 791965). *Parts, specifically TR6.*

Roadsters, Home Farm, Llanllawddog, Carmarthen, Dyfed (tel: 0267 253436). *Restoration.*

Classic Car Restoration and Repair, Bunas Park, Hollom Down Road, Lopcombe, Andover, Hampshire SP5 1BP (tel: 0264 781005). *Repairs and full restoration.*

Jim Hawkins (Trimming), 32A, Bridge St Mill Industrial Estate, Bridge St, Witney, Oxford (tel: 0993 778207). *All aspects of TR trimming.*

John Skinner (Trimming), 82B Chesterton Lane, Cirencester, Glos GL7 1YD (tel: 0285 657410). *All aspects of TR trimming.*

In the USA there are many firms providing repair and restoration services for TRs, but it is not practicable to attempt to list these here. Prospective customers are advised to contact the TR clubs in the USA for advice and details.

The following firms, amongst others, specialise in TR parts in the USA:

The Roadster Factory Inc, P.O. Box 332, Killen Road, Armagh, Pennsylvania 15920.

Moss Motors Inc, 7200 Hollister Avenue, Goleta, California 93117.